Attitools®

21 Attitools®
(ways of looking at things)

for

Personal Growth

for

*Darn near
anyone who breathes*

Ric Asselstine

Published in 1999 by
Ric Asselstine & Associates
Waterloo, Ontario, Canada

First Printing
August, 1999

Canadian Cataloguing in Publication Data

Asselstine, Ric, 1956-
Attitools: twenty-one ways of looking at things for personal growth
for darn near anyone who breathes

ISBN 0-9685740-0-9

1. Self actualization (Psychology) I. Title.
BF637.S4A82 1999   158.1   C99-901007-7

Although the author has exhaustively researched all sources to ensure
the accuracy and completeness of the information contained in this book,
we assume no responsibility for errors, inaccuracies, omissions or any
inconsistency herein. Any slights of people or organizations are
unintentional. Readers should use their own judgment and/or consult
an expert for specific applications of the material contained herein to
their individual situations.

All characters in this book are fictitious. Any resemblance to
actual persons, living or dead, is purely coincidental.

Photograph: Pirak Studios Limited
Cover Design and Typesetting: Suzanne Fournier
Production: Creative Options

Printed by Dollco Printing, Ottawa, Canada
First Printing 1999

To my family with love.

C O N T E N T S

the end

I said good-bye to a friend yesterday. We called him Counselor. That wasn't his real name, it was his nick-name. I met him ten years ago when he was my instructor at a training session. What he said that day affected me deeply. What he *gave* me that day changed my life!

Don't worry about our Counselor, though, he lived a great life, he *chose* to. Fact is, he croaked out joggin'. Eighty-five years old, ten below, boom; met his maker.

Said when he went, he wanted to go quick. He got his wish.

That's the way I want to go too. Heck, I'll take even being around at eighty-five. And thanks, at least in part, to what I learned that day, I think I'll have a way better shot at it. Because ten years ago he introduced us to a bunch of Attitools, his personal toolkit for everyday living.

I remember him always saying that he needed these tools more than anybody and that they'd helped him a lot. He constantly said his purpose was to humbly offer them up for our consideration. He didn't want to shove them down anybody's throat. But others told him they should be shared, so that's what he did.

I attended his funeral yesterday and flew back last night. While I was there, I saw Counselor's wife. I thanked her for sharing him with all of us. She had incredibly kind eyes.

She told me that, "as with all of us, his was not an easy life, but he *chose* for it to be a happy one."

I also saw a lot of the folks who were in that class with me those years ago, as well as many others his work had touched. Before we flew back, some of us had a chance to grab some dinner and get caught up. Man time flies!

It was great to see the others, to see how we'd all grown – in the good way of course – from having put these tools to use in our lives. So this morning I dug out my old Attitools workbook and started leafing through it. Thinking about that Saturday those ten years ago, I thought it only fitting that I revisit; that in honour of Counselor, I refresh my memory, to reflect on what he'd taught us.

I invite you to come along as I reminisce. You might be surprised at what happened that day...

---

lift off

Ten Years Before, At The Seminar....
Counselor strode briskly into the classroom. He then
turned to face us, to lift off the day.

Welcome to the Attitools Personal Growth Work
Session. I say *work session* because you will be *working*
today. The average adult attention span is less than one
minute and while I am *sure* you are exceptional adults, I
am *not* an exceptional speaker. *That's* why I need you to be
busy, he self-deprecated right off the bat.

Whenever I am in front of a class, there exists the risk
of severe and irreversible coma for those in attendance, he
joked, half serious, half not.

It has happened before, it could happen again. Not to
be concerned though. I have contacted the authorities to let
them know I am speaking today; they are therefore on full
alert! Most sleep medications have *nothing* on me, he
winked and fibbed. The pace he kept that day would make
those one-quarter his age sit up and take notice. He was
driven. We *would* learn that day and *he* would see to it.

He continued...

And these Attitools? I have used them for years. I use them everyday. I suspect I lean on them more than anyone.

They have added considerably to my level of hope and optimism; improved my outlook, my productivity, and my sense of control, and in so doing, have hopefully helped make me at least a little better husband, father and person. There is however, as you have probably already sensed, *vast* room for improvement. So while my *is* isn't my *could be* yet, it is much better than my *was*!

Say again?

While my *is* isn't my *could be*, he said once again slowly, it is better than my *was*.

As it turned out, *that* way of looking at things turned out to be his motto, his credo, *and* as it turned out, *his* wish for all of *us*.

He encouraged us to take comfort in the progress we make and then work to improve even further.

While we might not have it just right yet he told us, find peace in having come a long way.

Your *is* will not be your *could be* by the end of today, but my hope is that it will be better than your *was*.

And if I heard him say his motto once that day, I heard him say it a thousand times.

He was an interesting man. He didn't want to impose, yet, he wanted us to know what had ended up working for him.

I cannot know your reality, he observed correctly, that is not possible. We are the sole owners of our personal circumstances and our pasts. Only we know the joys and only we know the times we have suffered.

What has gone on in the past, we cannot change, however, how we look at it, can.

So, without regard to what our present and past lawns have looked like, I firmly believe we can all make the grass even greener as we go forward.

Brain jam. What was that? Analogy or metaphor?

No one was sure. We learned pretty quickly, though, that *neither* was he.

Counselor didn't speak English. He spoke a strange combination of analogy and metaphor to drive home his points. He spoke *Analaphor*! It drove his family crazy. It drove us a little nuts, too. But the more we fought through them, the more they made sense.

He called'em Analaphors, we fondly called'em brutal!

And the more we kidded him, the more comfortable he felt. The more we got to know him, the more *human* he became.

Coming back from the tangent, we were all settling in...

How we looked at things, before we came here, we cannot change. The perspective we leave here with, we most definitely can, he continued.

I am honoured that you chose to attend. And with that, he looked each of us in the eye, with a sincere look of thanks.

What to Make

That all took about thirty seconds.

I didn't really know what to make of Counselor at first. I was a bit cautious, like most folks, I guess. I didn't really know what we were in for. All I know is that by the end of that day *how* I was looking at things had changed drastically.

And how we looked at him had changed too.

Counselor

He was a distinguished older gentleman. Smartly dressed, tall standing, he even had a full head of hair.

He was dream driven yet reality-based, fiercely spirited and wise.

He was reserved, at first, but a friend by the end.

He was reassured for sure, but a little unsure at the start. He was constantly petrified that the points he was trying to make might not make their way through.

And as a result, our Counselor was *relentless*. *List* after *list*. *Analaphor* after *analaphor*. You couldn't get him to stop.

Are we clear on this? Are you OK with that? High-octane, his motor was always revved. *Get it, got it, good* was the only way he would let us press on.

He was the Head of Camp Saidanotherway he would tell us and *he* would decide the *helpings*. We rarely had to ask for *seconds*.

In fact, he would stalk around that room, almost in a prowl. High speed. Wincing. Hunching. Thumb, forefinger and middle finger on his left hand tri-scrunching in between his furrowed eyebrows. Eyes jammed shut. Grunting, angsting, he would search and search for that next best way to describe something, express something, portray something!

Sensitive to time but *needing* to be clear. Not wanting, or able from *his* perspective, to insult anyone's intelligence with his *ways of looking at things*, but wanting to be clear. *Never* wanting to offend, but always wanting to be clear. Never wishing to overstay his welcome but *needing* to be clear.

Thinking always thinking, dreaming always dreaming, he was humble to a fault, but he needed to be clear!

And all the while, while he went through these gyrations, we would politely sit there, a little bit amazed, having *gotten* what he wanted us to *get* the first time he would describe it, but watching in admiration as he did everything humanly possible to try to be of help.

And I think it was because of that; *because* he tried so hard and *because* he was *so* human and *because* maybe he *didn't* get it just right, that we warmed up to him so quickly. How could you not like this guy? Sure he'd mess up from time to time, but who of us doesn't?

He was a guy who was trying as hard at something as anyone I have ever seen.

He was genuine and well meaning, a little self-doubting but at peace all the same.

laying the groundwork

He pressed on to lay the groundwork...

There are twenty-one Attitools and we will cover them all today. My hope is that you understand each one before you leave.

I hope today serves as your "way of looking at things refueling station," he analaphored, flipping on an old gas station attendant's hat.

And that being the case, we simply can't go any further until we check your equipment, he said stopping abruptly.

Pardon?, we said.

Your equipment, what's under the hood, he clarified, we need to see how that engine's running. I can do this very quickly.

Uh, oh...

Please go to your Wiifm Scanner and check it for activity.

Our what?

Your Wiifm Scanner. Please let me explain...

A Wiifm Scanner is what we use to determine whether

or not we will *lock-in* and pay attention to something. It helps us determine whether something is worth listening to or not. As human beings, we have several *scanners* in operation at all times. Most times they run unconsciously, but they are *central* to how we behave. And a very powerful one of these scanners is our Wiifm Scanner, the *what's in it for me* scanner. It works constantly. It's *under the hood*. It looks for *now here's something worthwhile* blips to come across its screen. We need to ensure yours is working properly, so please check it, now. Anything showing up, anything registering?

Sure is, we played along.

Good, let's continue then, he said, straight-faced.

A seventy-five year old *kid*, this guy was, I recall saying to myself, a little surprised at first, but then a little envious.

Until, that is, he was able to get every one of us very much *into it*!

A Volunteer

Now, he said, peering out at us, I need a volunteer.

He grinned a mischievous grin as he scanned the room.

Our eyes shot straight down. Faster than his last investment, he joked. Half serious, half not.

None of us would lift up. You could *taste* the tension.

None of you wishes to volunteer?

I'm thinking, Geez, just give me a break, don't pick me. I'm wincing. And just then...

You there, Sir, he lasered. Yes, you!

You could just feel it. I raised my eyes slightly. Me?

Yes you, he continued quickly, how is Your Pomtgr? (pronounced PalmTiger)

Beg pardon?

Your Pomtgr.

Everybody in the room was staring at me, *pulling* for me...

Fine, I guess, how's yours, I spit out.

I'm glad to hear yours is fine and thank you for asking, my Pomtgr is fine. He's cool, calm and collected now. Settling in. He's got me, and us, right where he wants us.

By the way, do you know what a Pomtgr is?

Ah..........no Sir, I don't.

Well you are not alone. And thank you for putting up with my interrogation. It allows me to introduce the second in our family of scanners.

No sweat, I tell him. I'm drenched.

What we have just witnessed, he went on, was an illustration of an overactive Woptou Scanner.

A which?

A Woptou Scanner. A Woptou Scanner is what we leave on to gauge *What Other People Think Of Us*. Much like the Wiifm Scanner, it runs, most times, unconsciously. It can also override good judgment. It can stop us from asking for clarification because of what we believe other people might think of us, he declared, glancing my way, and smiling a thanks-for-being-a-good-sport kind of smile...

It is a feature that can be good, or a feature that can be bad. It is useful and wise to have *some* sensitivity to what other people think; for instance when we are about to meet our potential in-laws for the first time. But *too much* time spent on what others think of us lands us in the *keepin' up with the Jones's zone*. We end up making decisions based on what we think other people think, instead of on what we know to be right.

And that, he said, is not a good place to be. We end up doing things for the wrong reasons. We make bad decisions. We order power windows when we really don't need them for Goodness Sake, he kidded. Or more seriously, we might make decisions about what our kids can and cannot do based on what we believe others will think of *us*, as opposed to making decisions based on what we know to be right for the kids.

We should all behave according to Woptou sometimes; we need to get along, he acknowledged, but knowing that it exists now allows us to not *overbehave* according to it. Knowing that we have a tendency to do it at least allows us to not over do it.

I oughta know about this Woptou business, he said. I spent far too many years with an overactive Woptou and *still* do to this day.

But while my *is* isn't my *should be* yet, it's getting better than my *was*, pleased that he'd made progress while acknowledging that he still had a ways to go.

We were starting to *get* his approach...

Pressing On

Having cleared *that* up, let's get back to the main point, he said, the original point, what we are trying to accomplish here; let's get back to our Pomtgr!

Our Pomtgr is our Peace of Mind to Grief Ratio; an ultra-sensitive, scientific, here-for-your-eyes only, left-brain-accommodating measure of our overall well-being. It is what we are trying to improve here!

Our eyes are rolling now...

Like the Richter Scale and price-earnings ratio, it assigns a number to something. And in this case, that *something* is:

- our sense of well-being
- our hope versus our despair
- our desire to hop out of bed every morning
- our optimism versus our pessimism
- our positivity (Counselorspeak) versus our negativity
- our peace of mind to grief
- our overall, how are we doing

A high Pomtgr is good. A low one is not!

We get the picture. Our Pomtgr is a fun way of quickly expressing something that is central to our outlook, our overall well-being.

He then shifted from fun to serious...

As you know by now, I talk about these tools tongue-in-cheek. But the reality is that I could not take this work, these tools, more seriously. Because without these tools, I am not altogether sure that you and I would be meeting here today.

And the look on his face when he made that statement, left little doubt that what he *might* have meant by that statement, was *exactly* what he meant by that statement. These tools had literally helped him survive.

He paused, thinking deeply, and then pressed on...

You see, we land on this earth to do our best and to make our way here... To do a good job at what we do and to find happiness. And the world, if we look at it in a certain way, can present us with limitless opportunity. Viewed another way, it presents us with limitless grief.

And it is my conviction and my experience that *prop-*

erly equipped, the grief gives way to the opportunity. I have seen it, he said, and I have lived it!

Still sort of lost in thought, he continued. Slowly. Deliberately this time...

So if I seem relentless in our learning, if I stoop to any level to make things clear, if I seem like I just might *never* give up, it is because these tools are my *energy* and my *core*. It is because I know what can happen when we use them and I know what can happen when we do *not*, he said more forcefully than I think even *he* expected.

Collecting himself, he finished off...

These tools are born out of the frustration of *living* what it's like when we are ill-equipped and then seeing the improvement in our game that comes from *adding a new club or two to our bag*, he understated and analaphored all at once.

These tools may seem insignificant to some, he discounted, even childish to others, he gave away, but for me, they were life *changing*, and they are *all* I have to give, he laid bare.

The room went silent and time somehow stood still.

definitions

The preliminaries out of the way, the pace now quickened.

Most people have four questions they ask about these Attitools. What are they, what do they do, who can use them, and how are they used?

Allow me to clarify...

And with this, Counselor raced over to the overhead to display one of his many *lists*. And of course, because he was always in such a hurry, the slide would go up crooked or backwards. And of course, we would have to interrupt.

Counselor? The overhead?

Got it! Thanks...

And off he went.

Go. Go. Go. *Time* is *learning*, he would say, messing up the *old* adage, tossing these thoughts into the air for anyone to catch as he went about his business and then quickly pressing on, not waiting to see where they fell.

So what are Attitools, he asked rhetorically?

Attitools Are

- ways of looking at things that can be activated and deployed at will
- filters through which we view the world
- features we can add to our WorldProcessor
- ways of making sense of things
- tools for life planning, life management and *self-finetunement*
- mental processes we now raise to the level of consciousness
- ways to manage, upgrade and retrain *that voice inside*
- common sense formalized
- ideas to trigger our thinking

Attitools are perceptual tools or filters that allow us to see situations more clearly. *By raising to the level of consciousness the ways we think and perceive, we are better able to decide how we will act and behave.*

We already have most of these tools lying around in our mind, he said. In some cases we are already using them without even knowing we are using them. We might not be using all of them and the ones we are, we might not be fully exploiting.

Talk about disarray, he smiled...

A Distillery

I actually run a bit of a distillery here, he disclosed quietly, not just a little sheepishly, taking us into his confidence.

A distillery, certainly not you, Counselor! We were aghast!

Ssshhh, he ssshhhed, index finger to the lip.

Actually, it is a *way of looking at things* distillery, he continued. I have seen certain ways of looking at things that we use and we end up getting things right. I have also seen certain ways of looking at things that we use and end up getting things wrong. What I have simply done with Attitools is to raise these *ways of looking at things*, these patterns and processes, to the level of consciousness, and *distilled* them up for our use. By so doing, we learn to better use the ones that *work* for us and better *manage* the ones that don't.

I label these ways of looking at things and introduce you to some new ones as well.

So *what* can they do, he once again asked rhetorically? He put the next slides up a little more carefully...

Attitools Can Help Us
Survive
- help us with self-acceptance and self-understanding
- help us cope
- help us better manage and control how we analyze and see things
- help us carry on
- provide much needed reassurance that we are on the right track
- help us *better deal with* what happens to us, what people say to us and what people do to us
- help with how we communicate and relate to ourselves
- help us be objective when we need to be, more objective when it's tough to be
- comfort, console, reassure

Attitools Can Help Us
Learn
- help us understand why we do some of the things we do

- give people in relationships common ways of looking at things, to help us work things through
- offer clearer, more organized ways of looking at things
- help us better diagnose what's happening and better predict what could happen if we choose this or that
- help us recognize and better manage *the forces within*

Attitools Can Help Us
Prosper

- make better choices
- make better decisions
- strengthen our resolve
- reduce what appears to be random in our lives
- *plan* our own luck
- take charge
- make what was once ungraspable, graspable
- put us in the driver's seat

Attitools Can Help Us
Grow

- improve our Pomtgr
- help us close the gap between our *is* and our *could be*
- get us thinking
- *sand off a few coats of life* to get back to that original grain and texture
- get started
- keep going
- highlight where we need to make change
- be *kids* again
- *refresh* how we see things
- improve our relationships, with others and with ourselves

- improve communication
- be templates for change, at home and at work
- provide the contentment that frees up mindshare

He then walked us through who could use them.

Who Are They For?

Counselor told us he had been asked early on to define the types of people and situations where these tools could be used. He confessed that he had tried to narrow it down, but quite honestly could not.

So he took this issue to a group of his friends to see if they could help. In short order, they told him that these tools could be used by *darn near anyone who breathes* for *darn near any situation they find themselves in.*

Not disappointed with the outcome, he adopted this way of defining who they were for and how they could be used.

He then finished laying the groundwork by providing more detail.

How can we use them?

To Better Understand Why We Do The Things We Do

We all have consistent ways of thinking, behaving and managing our worlds. We all have consistent ways of looking at things. And by being aware of these patterns, by raising our existing patterns of thinking to the level of consciousness, we can see if they are working or whether there is room to improve.

We are many times on *auto pilot* with how we perceive and deal with things. Deploying these Attitools activates our manual override. Instead of *cruising*, we actively consider what we are doing along with how, and why. Looking through these filters, these Attitools, can provide us with clearer perspectives. And as a result, they can provide us with new and different alternatives for not only going forward, but also for making sense of what has happened in the past.

These filters, through which we can pass our life's circumstances, help expose the forces that drive our behaviour and drive our decisions. Using these tools, we can become more skilled at knowing why we and others do the things we and they do.

These tools help us do renovations, if that is what we choose.

Ten Pin Bowling Ball

Close your eyes everyone.

Come again? He caught us off guard. Every time Counselor asked us to close our eyes, he would change into one of his *getups*, but this was our first experience with it. He would switch off his Woptou Scanner and sacrifice a little dignity to reinforce our learning. He didn't mind coming off looking a *little* goofy if it meant we took more away from the day.

Fact is, he was a bit of a *ham* and the fact is, we ended up loving it.

OK, open 'em.

There he stood, in his professional bowler's shirt, complete with sponsors. He cupped a ten pin bowling ball in both hands.

Do you believe I can throw a strike with this ball? he asked, serious as heck, but looking a little weird.

Sure you can, Counselor, we cheered him on as he

began his wind up.

It is more likely though that I will throw a strike if what happens?, as he continued his pre-shot routine...

We don't know.

I am more likely to throw a strike if I am able to control the ball. I need to know where the holes are to put the proper spin on it. My likelihood of being successful will increase if I know how to control this thing!

Made sense.

Completing his backswing, the ball released! It smashed into the overhead projector...

Ooooops, didn't mean to let go. Happens every time. He had clearly *wasted* more than one overhead in his time.

Don't like overheads anyway, you could hear him mumble, bottom lip out...

A replacement was wheeled in...

The same goes for our behaviour, he continued. Once we can find the *holes*, the forces that drive our behaviour, we:

• can better control *the ball*, our behaviour, and the choices we make
• can better control our outcomes and our results
• can better control the ways we look at things

Once we find the *holes*, understand some of the processes, we are in a far better position to figure out why we may have had some *gutter balls*, made some mistakes or suffered some setbacks. Now we can be in a far better position, because we know how to control *the ball*, to hurl ourselves into the future, with a far better chance of making a strike, he analaphored, pretty well out of breath.

Some of us sat there once Counselor had finished *this*

little ditty and just smiled. He was goin' full out and some of it was even making sense.

As A Filter For Viewing Things More Clearly

An X-ray lets us see through. It lets us see things more clearly. Some Attitools serve as behavioural or situational X-rays.

When we break an arm or a leg, a doctor can take an X-ray and see the break clearly. Adjustments can be made to *lock in* the fix.

With *breaks* in our careers, our job, our relationships, up until now, it may have been difficult to *diagnose* what went wrong, to see what really caused or is causing the problem.

Some Attitools can be used to X-ray our breaks, to more accurately diagnose what is or was going wrong. To see where, and perhaps why, the break actually occurred. These tools, when deployed to analyze a situation, yield amazingly clear pictures of exactly where the break is or was. They can help diagnose why the problem might have occurred in the first place. And an accurate diagnosis typically leads to more focused treatment. We are then less likely to repeat our past mistakes or address the wrong problem.

Something about lessening the likelihood of going from the frying pan into the fire...

Deploying these Attitools can cause a state of *heightened awareness* of what causes things to go right in our lives and what causes things to go wrong, the upshot being the increased capacity to replicate and sustain "what's *right*" and be aware of and avoid those conditions in our lives that are causing "what's *wrong*."

The formalities completed, he kicked into high gear...

the worldprocessor

G one was the bowling outfit, he was now somewhere between an optometrist and a computer programmer; eye chart, jeans, personal web site, the whole thing. He was clearly ahead of his time.

How we act, react and behave grows out of *how* we interpret or process what is going on, he began. And it was this *interpretative process* with which he was so fascinated.

How can two people experience the same event and see it so differently, he wondered aloud? It is because *how* we perceive things differs so greatly from one person to the next, he concluded, answering for himself.

And the reason we perceive things so differently is because each of us has a one-of-a-kind, unique-to-each-of-us filter through which any event must pass before it registers.

And it was this filter or lens that Counselor called our WorldProcessor.

He called this filter a WorldProcessor (WP) because it shared many of the characteristics of a computer program.

And he said he knew *that* because he was Silicon Valley *connected*! We bought into the similarity part but weren't so sure about the connected part.

You see, we think our old Counselor may have been full of a little bit of *hooey*. Of course, he did nothing to discourage that notion.

If there *are* similarities between our personal processor and a computer program, and I believe there are, he continued, it logically follows that we can *revisit the program* running in our heads to change how we see things. We are free to do some reprogramming.

He knew it could be done. He had done it himself. He used these Attitools to upgrade *his* WorldProcessor. And it was this WorldProcessor concept that further laid the groundwork for *us* to go forward.

What Is Our WorldProcessor?

Our WorldProcessor (WP) is the filter through which we pass our life's events. It is how we *process* our world. It is the conscious/unconscious, formal/informal path that our life's events pass through as they *register* with us. *Our WP turns reality into our perception of it.*

It is what we use to decide how we are going to react to things. It is where we can embed our Attitools.

An Early Win

Counselor felt that *just knowing* we all have a WorldProcessor represented an early win. Stepping back just long enough to know that this process is deployed every time something happens, allows us the opportunity to study that process and to enhance it.

It is like knowing that an air filter exists in our car. Once we know it exists and that it affects our *perfor-mance*, we can just lift up the hood and check it, clean it, or change it, when need be, he said matter of factly, some-where out of nowhere.

Just knowing that we have this observable *unique-to-each-of-us* filtering process is significant, he said. Just knowing that this perceiving or WorldProcessing activity is functioning in us at all times makes this processing capacity easier to manage, and possibly easier to improve.

And *that* is what these Attitools are designed to do: to enhance our ability to *process* what is going on around us, thereby allowing us to make better decisions.

These Attitools are additional features that can be loaded in and added to our existing ways of looking at things; to upgrade, debug and strengthen our existing WorldProcessors.

With a computer program, he continued, the more powerful the program is, the better the results. The same goes for our WorldProcessor. The more clearly and comprehensively ours allows us to see things, the more effective we become!

We do things; we react, we act, we behave, we make decisions based on what our brain determines is happen-ing. So the better *equipped* it is, the more effectively it will function. The more *feature rich* and *robust* our WorldProcessor, the better we can make our way here!

Attitools are simply features we can add to our WorldProcessor to upgrade its processing power; features to help us see things differently, more clearly.

We can consciously activate and deploy them. Or, on occasion, they will even activate and deploy themselves, to our benefit, just when we need them, once we know they exist, he said, finally taking a breath.

And it was at *that* point that we were sure we had arrived at Camp Saidanotherway. We all knew we had such a filter. Only now it had a label. He then summarized our WP characteristics...

WorldProcessor Characteristics

- our WP's run largely in the background, possibly functioning autonomously, largely automatically
- our WP's have many features and components
- some features are running all the time and others need to be *clicked* on to activate
- our WP's need maintenance. Each WP can also be customized, enhanced, modified, and upgraded
- as with a computer program, our WP's may not be perfect
- we can activate and deploy WP features at will

Where Does the WorldProcessor Reside?

There is a place in between what happens to us and what we do about it. Our WorldProcessor resides in that space.

For some of us, this place is huge; we take our time, reflect and think before we act. For others, many of us, this place is small. We tend to act or react quickly, not knowing that we have the luxury, if we choose, to step back, evaluate and analyze what is happening before we decide what we are going to do. We simply react.

What Is Our WorldProcessor Made Up Of?

So what is our existing WP made up of? What are the *lines of code* that are now *installed*? What are the processing frameworks that have been added more unconsciously than consciously; the ways of looking at things that have *evolved* up to this point? What is our WorldProcessor made up of?

It is made up of where we have been. Our past roles and experiences. It comes from:

What We Have Learned

- the analytical tools, models and templates we have learned and used to analyze things up until now
- our existing frameworks for thinking; what we use to *break things down*, unbundle and make sense of them up to this point,
    and

What We Believe

- what we believe to be true about ourselves
- the perspectives and perceptions we have evolved
- our values
- what we believe to be important and what we believe to be unimportant
- our biases,
    and

The Choices We've Made

- the existing ways we *choose* to look at things

He purposefully let the word *choose* waft in the air because of its importance and then he continued...

So if these are our existing lenses, filters, windows, to the world, where then do we go from here, he asked?

We were confident that he had an answer.

As an optometrist can alter a prescription or a programmer fine tune his code, so too can we adjust how we see things, he told us. We can enhance the lenses we deploy and add to the tools that we have at our disposal. We can raise our WorldProcessor to the level of consciousness and upgrade it if we so choose. We can improve our *equipment.*

In fact, he proclaimed, we can actually learn how to self-optometrize! By changing our own lenses, we can learn to see things more clearly.

We smiled at that point and quickly turned the page.

the clicker

H is next *getup* was *cool*. Unmistakable.
Sweat pants, sweat shirt, baseball cap, a cold one in one hand. Unopened, of course. His ball cap scratching the top of his right temple, in the other hand. A look of utter confusion on his face as he faced the TV he had rolled in.

Honey, scratching away, Where's the Clicker?

Counselor *was* a real guy.

I give him credit. Seventy-five, and he's even got the bill curved just right. It even had a little sweat on it. Not bad.

You rock, Counselor!

It's right beside you Dear, he mocks himself.

He takes a look.

Oh Yeah, he finds it, visibly relieved.

The crowd likes this one. The guys are gruntin', ya got this one right buddy!

I thank you, he said stoically stepping in and out of character...

And why, you might ask, am I seeking a Clicker? The reason is that there is something we very much need to control. And what we need to control is *that voice inside*; the voice we listen to all the time. The one that:

- can be our best friend or our worst enemy
- can be our biggest fan or our harshest critic
- is the spokesperson for our WorldProcessor, the play-by-play announcer for how we are perceiving the world
- used to think, before now, that it could pipe up and say anything it wanted to and have us listen and pay attention
- tells us to *stew* or tells us to *stand easy*

It tells it like *it* sees it! Unfortunately, *how* it sees it isn't always right. Hence the need, at a minimum, for volume control. And what better way than with a Clicker?

Until such time as we can perhaps give *that voice inside* a different way of looking at things, which will be by the end of today, Counselor assured us, we need to figure out a way to at least control its volume. And while the *Mute button* on the Clicker that's hooked up to *our voice inside* doesn't *always* work, we can turn the volume down a little, anyway.

We therefore need to install the Clicker into our WorldProcessor right off the bat. Right now.

Counselor told us that the quality of what he said to himself, the quality of *his* voice inside, had improved in lockstep with *how* he *learned* to look at things. As he upgraded his WorldProcessor, his ability to see things differently and a little more clearly, the quality of his internal narrative followed.

And because *that voice inside* only *calls it as it sees it*, we need to help *what* it sees and *how* it sees it. Once we strengthen our way of perceiving things, what we say to ourself and how we say it, improves.

This *voice inside* is another *built-in/preinstalled* feature of our WP. We can rarely hear it on the outside. The exception being when we are on the golf course and we mis-hit our ball.

Listen carefully right at that moment, he said. Right then you might get a rare glimpse of the *evil side* of the *voice inside*. It emerges/presents itself at that very moment in the form of a SLOMOE. A Self-Loathing Muttering Of Exasperation.

These mutterings are highly personal, usually hilarious and directed at ourselves in a kidding, but not kidding, sort of way. They range from *I hate me* to *you got what you deserved*. They are clear evidence of internal dialogue. But not the kind we want!

That voice inside is hard to hear on the outside, thank goodness he said, but can't *not* be heard most times on the inside. Hence the need for the Clicker and a WP upgrade. It's *there* so why not improve what it says.

We can learn to turn it down when we gotta, and turn it up when we oughta! He smiled proudly at his new invention.

It's just something we need to be aware of. It is also something we can learn to manage better. We can control it as opposed to having it control us.

And now that this dimension of our behaviour, this feature of our WP, is exposed, and *raised to the level of consciousness*; with the assistance of some additional tools, we should be able to turn it from a potential antagonist into a trusted ally. From a heckler into a fan. From issuing SLOMOEs to providing guidance and support. From *you got what you deserved* to *you still Da Man*!

Now that would be more like it...he trailed off and smiled having misplaced his Clicker and therefore having to beat back a SLOMOE of his own.

Again.

the preflight checklist

This is your Captain speaking!
He was into a new getup. He had the hat on, the wings on his collar, the whole nine yards. And he was standing just outside the *cockpit*, facing us, kind of puffed up, trying to look official.

Before this plane takes off, we need to check our flight readiness. Our capacity and willingness to accept and make change. Our willingness to consider new ways of thinking; the extent to which we are capable of installing new tools in our WP.

Because you are *here*, though, I presume that I am preaching to the converted. I presume you are already *good to go*! However, in my job, you can never be too careful, hiking up his trousers, looking, unfortunately, much more like a Leslie Neilson character than the 'fighter pilot' look he was after, but nobody said anything.

So, to assess *flight readiness*, I have developed a checklist to help recognize some of the reasons we sometimes find it hard to *get airborne*.

I use these ways of looking at things to help me understand why I might not be making headway from time to time, he said. It serves as a healthy audit list.

There are all kinds of reasons why we occasionally can't get off the ground, why we don't make change. Here are some of them:

We Simply Don't Want To Change

Some folks are just plain *fed up*. They've had it. They're worn down. They *may* even have a condition called psychosclerosis. Hardening of the attitudes. Psychosclerosis is a condition that evolves over time. Life's events can erode our desire and willingness to change over time and erode our openness to things.

We got the point. Some of us had seen people like that. Sometimes we had even seen that person in the mirror.

We Are Creatures Of Habit

We are creatures of habit. We stick with what works for us and embed it into how we operate; how we think, and how we act. We develop these habits consciously or unconsciously, and as with cholesterol, they tend to build up.

As with cholesterol, he pressed on, on very thin medical ice, not all habits are bad, he backtracked, like putting on a seat belt, or flossing, or doing pushups, there are good habits. It's just we that oughta know what habits we have, that's all!

He was tri-scrunching again, but he was making sense...

A classic example of habit is our morning routine, he went on as he invited us to consider how much of our day we can actually go through, more or less on autopilot, without having to make a single decision.

We *are* creatures of habit. And *that*, sometimes is why we tend to avoid change. It also sheds some light on why it is tough to make change.

We Don't Know We Need To Change

Reason three for not changing is we don't know we need to. Diagnosis? Boiled frog syndrome.

What is that?

Some had heard of it before, so he gave the quick version. Frogs can't sense gradual temperature change. Throw them in a pot and crank up the heat and sadly, they will boil. They are unaware that the world around them is changing and that they ought to do something about it.

Counselor could be pretty direct when he wanted to be.

Same thing occurs with us. Conditions around us can change constantly. Our world can change and sometimes we don't sense it.

And that is *not* a good thing!

We Don't Know We Are Capable of Making The Change

Another reason we tend not to change is that we self-constrain; we self-limit. *We* determine that we can't make *that* change. *It's not in us.* We don't believe we can do it. We constrain ourselves because of what *we* believe to be true about ourselves; our capabilities, our limitations, and our beliefs around what is possible.

And then we forget to check those beliefs for validity.

And as we well know, what we believe pretty well amounts to what we do. Or don't do! It amounts to whether we give ourselves clearance to take off or not.

Many times, *we* hold us back. If we believe we can't, we won't.

However, if we believe there is a way, there can be a will.

We Don't Know What Is Possible

The next reason Counselor touched on as to why we don't change or don't seek to try, is that we either *don't know to* or *don't think to* explore what is possible. We don't think to explore what a raised bar looks like; what we *really can* accomplish.

Not the *bar* bar kind he admonished, the high jump bar, he huffed, a little frustrated that this analaphor had missed the mark slightly.

When we *know* what is *possible*, our capabilities are unleashed. When we *know* what *really good* is, we are far more likely to *take it up a notch* and actually get to what *really good* is.

Lots of Reasons

There are all kinds of reasons not to change, he pointed out. Fact is, there is a list of *reasons not to change* already embedded in our existing WP. Some come from the head—no time, don't know how. Some come from the heart—no one in my family has ever accomplished *that* before.

Some are rational and some are not. But the point is, they exist.

And the suggestion here is to *know* that they exist! And then to ensure that these reasons don't deploy themselves *automatically*, seizing us up before we even give something a chance. Because it is when we start to *automatically* recoil in the face of change, when we *auto-eject* in the face of *new*, that we know that our wings are beginning to ice up, analaphors flying.

When the thought of change triggers an immediate *I don't think so* response, without fair consideration, we *know* we are seizing up!

Thankfully though, now that you are aware of all of this, if a *chronic resistance to change* even *starts* to build up in any of us, we will immediately hear an audible DANGER, DANGER, DANGER.

It will sound exactly the same as when Robot went crazy on *Lost In Space*, as it regularly did. Once that *DDD Alarm* goes off, your WP will then automatically reconfigure itself to being incredibly receptive to change.

Oakey Doak?

Oakey Doak, Counselor.

Counselor said the only reason he knew about Robot was because he allowed his children to watch the show when they were younger due to its educational value.

We teased him because we figured he just had a crush on Maureen.

He blushed, but continued.

Being receptive to change is a very good thing, he reminded us. We live longer. We learn more. We remain vibrant and it feels good when we try. We stay with the times and our kids like what they see.

The Upshot

So the upshot? The upshot is that there are always good reasons to stay in steady state. There are, however, even more compelling reasons to look positively at change, to explore what is possible. Yes it can be frightening, and yes it can be painful, but the benefits of embracing change, in my experience, far outweigh the costs.

Of that, he was sure.

Mission Control

And with that, he had somehow morphed! No longer was he a fighter pilot wannabe. In his mind and with his demeanour, he was now our Mission Control Specialist, space-rigged headset and all! He said the headset was authentic too!

No matter, it was time to lift off!

He was about to conduct the required *preflight readiness roll call*. And *we* were at the controls!

I have now completed my preflight checklist, he reported. You have all passed. Your obvious willingness to embrace change has earned you the right to proceed.

We nodded in the affirmative. We were about to earn our wings, about to take off.

He read out each of our names as a sort of right of passage into Attitooldom.

It was crazy, but I didn't care. I *was* at *Mission Control* and if he thinks he's in Houston, then I can sure as heck take flight!

When he came to each of us though, I have to tell you, we each seemed to sit up a little straighter.

Then, he stood before me.

You, sir.

Yes, sir.

Good to grow?

Roger that Flight!

We exchanged salutes.

Lift off!
Get it?
Got it.
Good.
We proceeded.
Crisply.

the knife

C lose your eyes he said....we had achieved lift-off.
OK, Open'em!

There he stood, a cross between a French Chef and an Outback mate. He had this Chef's hat on and a pasted moustache, patched crooked on his lip, that kept threatening to dislodge. He carried a menu in one hand and one big honkin' machete in the other.

The Ingredients

I wish to tell you a story. I will do so in a roundabout way.

As if you could do it any other way, we chided him.

He smiled, but this one was serious.

Let me begin by saying that there are a total of one hundred *ingredients* in three categories—job content, job context and life context, that combine to make up our *recipe* of life's circumstances. We come into contact with most of these *ingredients* every day. We *experience* them regularly. We *taste* them every day.

We are served these ingredients based on the choices we

make, where and whom we work with, and where and whom we live with. And these ingredients affect how we feel.

Some of these ingredients energize, some drain. The rest fall somewhere in-between. The point though is that *we* author the recipe. *We* create our own menu. *We* decide what the ingredients are. *We* make the choices.

Let me come at this another way, he said.

The Effect

Based on the life decisions we have made, the jobs we have chosen, where we live, we taste the effects of these choices every day.

Some of these *things* affect us positively and some negatively. Some of these *things* have a huge impact on us. Others are less significant. Some we control outright. Others we have less influence over. Some will change. Some won't.

There is, however, a cumulative effect from all of these ingredients. These ingredients affect our overall well-being, our Pomtgr.

And because we are the *chef*, we can control what's on the menu every day, what the ingredients are. We, therefore, control our own well-being and our own Pomtgr.

At least that was his reasoning. And at this point, we would go along with him, but we needed more on this one before it got the stamp of approval, which it ultimately, most definitely, did.

How we ultimately feel is driven by the choices we have made and continue to make, he added. Some of us are satisfied with the way we have configured our life's ingredients. Some of us are not.

The trick then, he said, is to identify those specific

ingredients in the recipe that don't taste right and deal with them. And to figure out which ones are adding significantly to the taste on the positive side and hold them constant.

Plain English

Let me step outside the Analaphor for a moment. I want to get this just right, he said.

This must be important, we figured.

This will be our longest section of the day. It is, however, one of the most important. If you hang in with me though, I think you will be amply rewarded.

We gave our heads a little shake to keep the blood flowing and then settled in...

Alright.

When I talk about these ingredients, I am talking about things in our lives that affect us on a day to day basis; the jobs we've taken, where we've decided to live, how we spend our time and who we chum with.

And while all of these things seem to be interrelated, to a large degree, they *can* be split out. In fact, they *need* to be split out if they are to be properly analyzed to determine their effect. They need to be looked at individually to fully appreciate the impact they are having on us.

Chop It Up

And as a result of personal experience and having coached, counseled and interviewed all kinds of people, it has become quite evident that the extent to which we can *unbundle* our lives; the extent to which we can understand what is going on, is the extent to which we can have peace and make the right choices.

The extent to which we can break our life's circumstances down into their component parts, to figure out and isolate exactly which parts are working and which parts need attention, is the extent to which we can make the proper adjustments, while keeping what works intact.

It is the extent to which we can open up the hood, and look at the parts to see which ones are working and which ones need repair, that we are better able to make the trip from Intensity to Easygoing, he said, getting way ahead of himself.

Looking At The Recipe and Its Ingredients

There are three major *slices*/layers/life components/areas where we need to focus. And within those three areas, there are a total of one hundred ingredients we need to be sensitive to. And it is this list of ingredients that make up our daily recipe, our daily diet of experiences, that by the end of the day either leave us feeling energized, drained or somewhere in between.

Some of these *ingredients* bring us pleasure and some bring us pain. These ingredients represent our control panel. And once we know what they are and the effect that each has on us, we can retain the ones that affect us positively and deal with the ones that affect us negatively; either changing them or changing how we feel about them.

Raising each dimension to the level of consciousness; pulling each part out of the engine out for a *looksee*, to look at it, analyze it and assess its impact on our day to day outlook, can cause a few forehead slaps. It is sometimes like, *Wow, I hadn't really looked at my life like that before*, I hadn't really realized that there were all of these things that could affect my mood and I certainly didn't realize the effect that *that* was having. And I definitely had lost sight of the fact that much of what went on occurred because of the decisions *I* had made.

This is the type of impact this way of looking at things had on me, he said.

And what is the long and the short of it? If we conduct a thorough analysis of the ingredients affecting us, we can improve our recipe. And hence, our Pomtgr reading. We can modify what doesn't taste right and maintain or add more of what does.

This one hundred point *viewing filter* allows us to *identify and label* the ingredients in our recipe quite easily. The *Famous One-Hun* as I call them serves as a checklist we can use to look at the different aspects of our lives to check off which ingredients add positively and to dog ear the ones that need work.

I now introduce this way of breaking things down to you for your use....as he picked up his *knife*...

The Famous One Hun

So let's identify and name the famous one-hun, he enthused in his best Aussie accent. Problem was, he looked more like an all-thumbs chef's apprentice with the knife than he did an Outback pro. Just a little awkward with his cutting instrument...

Let's do some slicing! Let's slice our life into sections, unbundle it, break it down into its component parts, identify the ingredients...

The Slices Of Life

There are three main slices of our life where our ingredients, the famous one-hun, reside. The three *slices* are:

Our Job Content—what we do in our jobs, our job duties, and what those duties require of us.

Our Job Context—the setting in which we do our jobs.

Our Life Context—our personal life, our home life, our non-work life.

These are the *big three*. This is how we break it down. These are the three filters through which we can now view our world to unbundle it and figure out which ingredients energize and which ingredients drain.

Clarity

Splitting our life's circumstances into these three distinct categories lets us see our lives in three dimensions (*3D*)—job content, job context and life context—and allows us to view them with increased clarity and then start to make the needed changes.

You don't put a cast on your arm if you've sprained your ankle, Counselor blurted out of nowhere. This way of looking at things just helps us *zero in* more accurately on *where the hurt is*. If the job content is the issue, design the fix for that ingredient. If there is a job context stone in your shoe, deal with that!

It is like *finding the holes in the bowling ball*. Remember, he said, taking us back to the intro...

We can now better control it. We can finally identify, figure out, lock in on those things that *most* affect how we are feeling and do something about them. And with this level of detail, we are able to do so with the type of precision that we might not have contemplated before. It is like being given a laser to do surgery as opposed to a hand axe. It just lends itself to more precision.

A little graphic don't you think Counselor?

Anything to make a point, he said, as he picked up the knife again.

We recoiled in mock, or at least *sort of*, mock horror.

What we do about or how we feel about each of these ingredients is adjustable and/or controllable. As I mentioned before, we *can* change the recipe.

Consequences

There are however consequences and repercussions associated with every adjustment we make. As you know from physics, he said, for every action, there can be an equal and opposite reaction. *Change even one ingredient in the recipe and you will change the taste.*

We were clear.

Decisions, Decisions

He also suggested that while it is true that we can decide how we feel about anything, it just makes sense to create circumstances and place ourselves in the circumstances that we know are a fit and that naturally yield positive outcomes. It takes the decision making about how we are going to feel about something out of the loop. We know we are going to feel good because we have created the life circumstances (job content, job context, life context) that work for us. There is no decision making involved.

Feeling good/having peace of mind is the natural result, not a forced reaction.

Common Sense

Counselor had experience with this...

Early in my career, he said, I spent way too much time and emotion, griping about *how I felt* about things and *not nearly enough* time doing something about the *things that caused me to feel that way.* I *had* been spending way too much time thinking a fix was out of my hands and not nearly enough time fixing the problem. I was bailing water when I should have been patching the hole.

Must have been an equipment thing, he smiled.

Now I understand *why*, though. Before I had a vague feeling about what was right and what wasn't working. I then evolved the *tools* to do a proper analysis; to see *exactly* where there was something that needed to be fixed.

I had also forgotten that it was *me* who had made all the choices that had lead me to how I felt. No one had forced me. That said, though, I also realized that because I had made choices, it also meant that I was free to continue to make choices; about how I felt, what I did and how I could continue to evolve my life *and* my life's circumstances.

I couldn't change what had gone on before. But I could most definitely change what went on from here!

So that is what I did, he concluded.

Diagnostic and Predictive

Counselor also pointed out, and this was important,

that we can *take a snapshot* to analyze/better understand any period in our life using this three-sliced, one-hundred-dimensioned analytical filter. We can look back at the various eras in our lives and learn more from them.

Ask yourselves...

What types of job content usually worked. What about job setting? What types brought out the best in us and what types brought out the worst? We can then use the knowledge gained from this diagnosis to better predict the 3D configuration that will yield the optimal results. Young folks, even all of us, can look at summer jobs as a start. Which parts did we like and which parts didn't work?

This way of looking at things can also allow us to look at possible *future* job/life configurations a little more objectively. We can look at these situations using the *famous one-hun* and square that with what we know about ourselves having looked at the past. And by so doing we can make a fairly accurate *educated guess* about whether what we have in mind is going to work or whether it is not.

Using this diagnostic filter, we can better predict future outcomes. We can *scan it through this Attitool* to better see if it is likely to work.

It was now time to unveil the *famous one-hun.*

Three Slices Break Into One Hundred

Let's now have a look at the *famous one-hun.* The job content slice has thirty ingredients, the job context slice, fifty-two and the life context slice twenty-three ingredients totaling one hundred and five. The math didn't work, but Counselor wasn't strong on detail. It was somehow "a hun" to him...

THE JOB CONTENT SLICE

The job *content* slice lets us unbundle our job to help us figure out if our job requirements let us do what we like and are good at. The probes, or filters, we go through allow us to look at any job situation to determine *fit*.

Here are the *job content ingredients* in our recipe.

1. Am I using the skills and abilities I like to use, want to use and am good at?
2. Do I have a *knack* for doing what this job requires me to do?
3. Are there parts of the job that I am good at and parts that I am not?
4. To what extent am I a *natural* for this? Is this job *me*? Does this job *fit* me?
5. Am I going with my strengths?
6. Do I intuitively know what I am supposed to do next or do I constantly have to ask?
7. Do I just *know* who my customers are and what they want or do I struggle a bit as I look around?
8. Am I proud of what I am doing?
9. Do I think what I am doing is important?
10. Is my job satisfying?
11. Am I learning and growing? Am I *interested*? Am I fascinated? (The more of each of these in particular, the *tighter* the fit.)
12. Can I see the effect or impact of what I do?
13. Can I see the effect or impact of what I do on the big picture, on other people?
14. Is that important to me or is it not an issue?
15. Just by doing my job, do I know if I'm doing a good job? (Brain surgeons, as an example, know when they are

having a good day and definitely know when they are not.)

16. Again, is knowing important to me or am I OK not knowing?

17. Does this job let me be creative to the extent that I want to be?

18. Am I using the breadth or variety of skills that I like to use? Too many, too few, or well within my zone of reasonableness?

19. Can I pretty well decide when and how to get the job done or is that decided elsewhere? Regardless of where these calls are made, am I OK with how much decision making latitude I have?

20. Is the job fun? To what extent is this a hoot?

21. What parts of the job are fun? What is a hoot? And what parts are like having a tooth filled?

22. What parts of this job would I do for free?

23. What parts give me the willies, cause me angst, use my least evolved strengths, expose my weaknesses, the things I can't do and have no interest in learning?

24. Does the job require the level of effort, both physical and mental, that works for me right now?

25. Does the job yield the amount and type of people contact I am after, with suppliers, customers, coworkers, my boss?

26. By doing my job, am I learning the types and amounts of things I want to learn?

27. To what extent am I enveloped by an area that I find of interest?

28. Do I know *exactly* who my customers are?

29. Am I pleased with the quality and quantity of work I am able to produce?

30. Are my customers satisfied?

These *probes* allow us to analyze the extent to which the duties we are performing yield the types of outcomes we are after. Does the job work for us or does it not? What parts of it are a fit and what parts are a stretch?

THE JOB CONTEXT SLICE

As with job content, we similarly feel the effects on a day to day basis of the *setting* in which we do our jobs. And that is job context.

He went on to point out that the area of job context was the area around which he had focussed a lot of his attention. Many times, most times, we think in terms of our working life or our jobs as being one-dimensional. In fact, you now know that that could not be further from the truth. Our job is made up of what we do *and* the setting in which we do it. And each can have a significant impact on our overall well-being.

He was clearly speaking from experience here. The stuff we do in our jobs, he said, the job content, tends to be a real source of satisfaction. It is *what* we do. It is the setting in which we do our job, however, that can, sometimes cause problems. The potential exists for the job context to be enriching and energizing, but that requires the knowledge that it exists and the willingness to attend to it. It can also severely drain.

So you leaders, managers and coaches out there *better know that*. Because it is largely you who sets the context and set the tone for the people that work with you. You set it by what you do and what you say, what you measure and what you ignore. He stated this in no uncertain terms, getting a little ahead of himself.

He wouldn't let the rest of us off the hook either, though.

The organization may set the context, but it is up to us to determine the fit.

Pretty strong words from a guy who, on the strength of this knowledge, had finally learned how to relax.

He then smiled rather knowingly, knowing the point he was about to make would hit home.

Full snort, real proud of himself, Barney Fife-like, inverse shoulder-roll and simultaneous britch-hike, he proceeded...

When looking at job context, it's like, he said, pausing for even more effect, *you marry the person, you marry the family*! And in some cases, as you know, that can be good, and in some cases, that can be bad.

He collected himself pretty quickly though, assuring us that in his particular case he could not have been more fortunate. He was no dummy.

You take the job, you get the setting. Job setting ingredients can energize or they can drain. And what's interesting is that *what energizes one person can drain another.* Hence the *need to know context* and the *need to know ourselves.*

Once again, he was getting ahead of himself...

Here are the *job context ingredients* in our recipe. And each has either a direct or indirect impact on whether or not we fit.

The Business

1. Are we interested in what our organization does?
2. How do we like the *pace*? Is the company growing or not? Is this an issue for us? Is it a competitive business or not? Is the industry we're in stable or is it changing every day? How does what we need and enjoy right now square with all of that?

3. Am I interested at a gut level in the industry itself and in what we do?
4. Do I read industry or trade magazines just for fun?
5. Is my training, education and experience generally in the same area as those in positions where I have aspirations?
6. Do I intuitively understand the industry and business and how it works, who the *players* are and how to improve it?
7. Am I naturally interested and proud of the industry?
8. Do I know who our customers are and why they are buying from us?

My Work Setting

9. What is my work setting *like*? The features/characteristics/make-up of my physical work space (chair type and angle, time spent sitting/standing, desk, tools, proximity to others, walls, light, heat, etc).
10. Does my work setting energize or drain?
11. What parts of it energize and what parts drain?
12. How is my daily commute?
13. How about business travel, amount, type, etc, and how is that affecting me? Good, bad, indifferent?
14. And creature comforts; *facilities*, access to food, cleanliness. Are they acceptable or unacceptable?
15. What is the time and distance to the nearest Tim Horton's (Counselor couldn't resist...)
16. Physical setting ingredients to factor in: noise levels, colours, decorations, lighting, temperature.

Rewards

18. How am I compensated and how does that square with

what I need, prefer, or want?

19. Is the *comp plan* in line with *how* I like to get paid? Straight salary, hourly, commission, base pay, a combination, bonus, profit sharing?
20. Am I being paid fairly?
21. Is money an issue or am I OK?
22. Am I getting the other types of rewards I am after? Recognition?
23. If I overperform, am I rewarded?
24. If I underperform, do I hear about it?
25. Are the rewards, monetary and non-monetary, fair and equitable across the board, to the extent that they can be? Are we inside or outside our zone of reasonableness?
26. Are the benefits, vacation, health benefits, etc., in line with where our family needs them to be right now?

Policies

27. Am I OK with the rules that govern where I am at; hours of work, flexibility, dress code, parking, security, health and safety?

Leadership

28. Am I OK with how my leaders; my direct boss and the other leaders in the organization, lead?
29. If they tell, ask, involve, explain, order, praise, direct, support, ignore, criticize, evaluate, cheerlead, is that the type of leadership style I work best with or can tolerate or, once again, is this an issue that doesn't really affect me, because not all ingredients affect everyone?
30. If the prevailing leadership style doesn't square right

now, is it likely to change over time?

31. How does the level of feedback I get square with what I want or need?
32. Do I get clued in? Am I able to clue myself in to the extent that I want to be or need to be right now?
33. Do I know where I stand to the extent that I need to and want to?
35. Am I able to provide input to the level where I am comfortable and is it received in a way that works for me?

The Organization's Culture

36. Does the mood, personality, "the way we do things around here", square with my values and the way I like to do things?
37. Do I admire, trust, respect and can I relate to the founder, president, leader?
38. Is that important to me right now?
39. Is what is important, measured and paid attention to by the leaders important to me? Are we aligned? And again, is that an issue for me?

Growth Setting

40. Will the setting that I am analyzing provide the types of growth opportunities I am after; chances to learn more, earn more, travel, etc.?
41. Can I build the experience and develop the skills I want to?
42. Do others expect too much, too little or just the right amount of me? Am I being stretched, staying in steady state or falling behind? And again, is this something that is a real issue for me right now or is it on the back burner for the moment?

How We Communicate

43. Is the way we communicate around here the way I like to communicate and am comfortable with?
44. Is the level of communication around here in line with what I need right now?
45. Am I comfortable with how and when I communicate with those I need to communicate with; coworkers, customers, suppliers, my boss?

Technology and Equipment

46. Do I have the tools I need to do my job, to serve my customers, to meet their needs?
47. Do I have a knack for using the types of technology I am required to use in my job and my work setting?

People Contact

48. Do those people whom I come into contact with at work energize, drain or do neither?
49. Are those I associate or come into contact with adding to my overall sense of well-being or taking away? Put more succinctly, am I *allowing* those with whom I come into contact or associate with at work, to energize or drain?

Amount of Risk

50. Am I OK with the amount of risk, stability, security this work setting offers?
51. What are the chances of a layoff? Is this an issue or am I OK with where all of this is at?
52. Does any of this cause me to lose sleep or does where I am provide the level of stability I can live with?

And these, ladies and gentlemen, are the job context ingredients it helps to know about. They are included in most of our recipes.

There was more around job context, however, that he was anxious for us to know...

The Evolution of Job Context

Counselor wanted to touch on his take as to why and how job contexts evolve. His experience and research had lead him to conclude that contexts evolve for a reason. They don't evolve randomly or haphazardly, rather, they evolve to *best meet the objectives of a given organization.*

If we wait for an organization's context to *come around* to what works for us, we might be waiting for quite some time, he submitted politely.

Let me clarify, he said.

The job context or setting of any organization evolves to what it ought to be, to better facilitate results, outcomes. It evolves to what allows the organization to best meet its objectives, not necessarily to what makes all of us happiest, although that is the win-win that is ideal.

Moreover, it is what it should be and for very good reasons. It evolves to what it ought to be to enable the organization to best do what it is trying to do. Different organizations, at different stages, with different motives (profit driven or not for profit) will naturally evolve different settings or job contexts to best meet their objectives.

Our task is to find the content and context that fit us best!

The context will be what best allows the organization to do what it *needs* to do. Which, he pointed out is not a bad thing. It is simply what it is. And it is important for us to know that, he reiterated.

I think the voice of experience was coming out again...

We can spend a lot of time wishing for closer alignment between our *is* and our *wish to be* job context. Or we can accept the reality that a misalignment, if there is one, is no one's fault. Many times it grows out of not knowing that different types of organizations will have different types of work settings/job contexts.

And once we accept that, we can either accept far more easily where we are at, acknowledging a discrepancy between our *is* and *would like to be* if there is one, or, we can evolve our reality over time. We can gravitate toward a job, or a department or a department leader that creates the type of context we work best in. No knee jerk, just orderly progression.

It can and does take time. But at least *the choice* is under our control. And once again, just knowing that the ball is in our court, and perhaps knowing better now how to put together a game plan, we can reduce some uncertainty and send ourselves spinning more accurately toward our desired ten pin, he multi-analaphored.

Some Rules of Thumb

For your consideration, there are some rules of thumb that I have evolved over time to help me deal with job contexts. These are more observations than anything, he said, but they have worked well for me:

- larger, older organizations have set ways
- smaller, newer organizations are finding their ways
- the closer the organization is, or feels, to the customer, the more vibrant the setting

- larger organizations seek specialists while smaller organizations need generalists
- the more competitive the business, the more outward the focus
- if we want to understand what a job setting is likely to be, look first at what the organization is trying to accomplish, and *then* look at the values of those leading
- if we want to know the mood of the department, look first to the person who runs it and then what the department is trying to accomplish

So, by looking at and, assessing:

- the size
- the age
- the extent to which it has to fight to survive
- the aggressiveness and number, if any, of its competitors
- the values and actions of the leaders

of an organization or department, we can gain insight into what its work setting is likely to be.

For example, we will know that a start-up technology company will have a far different work setting than a mature government department. And that is neither a good thing nor a bad thing. That is just the way it is. Each organization will have a job context that best enables it to accomplish what it is trying to accomplish. And there is some degree of comfort in knowing that.

The context or *feel* of a place can even vary by department. What works for Production may not work for Research & Development. So while the company mandate and leaders will establish the colour, different shades can and do appear across departments. And there is some comfort in knowing that, too.

What This Means

What this means is that we now have the *tools* to better predict the type of context an organization is likely to have. We are therefore, better able to make a judgment about whether a given setting could represent a *fit*.

Three Nines and Two Tens

Counselor then told us a cute little story to help put this to bed.

When I was a kid, he began.

You were a kid once? we kiddingly interrupted him.

Why *yes,* I was, he shot back, taking mock offence.

When I was a kid, he began again, I used to play cards, Euchre, with my grandmother. And I distinctly remember one evening being dealt three nines and two tens.

For those of you who play Euchre, you know that three nines and two tens is darn near grounds for a mis-deal. So, of course, I whined and complained. My Grandmother, of course, would have none of that and proceeded to whoop me, in the card game, of course...

She did, however, point out to me, as she marked five for her and none for me, that while three nines and two tens is not good in Euchre, it is *very* good in poker. A full house in poker, she said, is *never* a bad hand.

So' twas a good hand you had son, just the wrong game!

And that Counselor told us was a very good lesson! We are all dealt very good hands. The *trick* is to find the right game!

'Nuff said?

'Nuff said.

One more major slice to go.

Hangin' in?

Hangin' in.

THE LIFE CONTEXT SLICE

The *third set of ingredients* come from our life context, our home life, our non-working life, what we do before work and after.

The life context slice you will recall, has twenty-three ingredients. And as with job content and job context, we feel the effects of the life context choices we've made and make, every day. These ingredients can add tremendous richness to the taste or they can affect us negatively.

Some would argue that these ingredients are the *most* important, the ones that *really* matter, the ones that ought most closely be managed and attended to, he observed. And with that he presented the list of *life context ingredients*.

Our Family Life

1. How are things going at home; our relationships with spouse, kids, parents, in-laws?
2. And how about friends and other relatives? Are these relationships working and energizing or are there bumps in some of these roads?

Our Health

3. What kind of shape are we in?
4. Are we making choices that will have us stick around for a while or are we headed for early checkout?
5. What are my eating habits?
6. What are my vices?
7. How much and how well am I sleeping at night?

8. What is my exercise regimen?

Our Finances

9. How are we doing dough-wise?
10. Is where we are at a cause of concern, a preoccupation, or are we on track?
11. Do we have some form of retirement plan or are we still helping the kids with school?
12. How are all of these things affecting us?

Our Spirituality

13. Are we at peace with our maker?
14. Are we where we want to be here?

Our Spare Time

When we got to this part everybody chuckled. What spare time?

15. Are we taking any time for ourselves?
16. If so, what are we doing with it?
17. Does what we do, and who we do it with, in our spare time energize or drain?
18. Am I taking any courses, learning, volunteering, giving back?

Where We Live

19. Does where we live contribute positively to our overall well-being or is there a gap for now?
20. Are we close enough to family or too close?
21. Is where we live vis-a-vis all the things we are trying to accomplish—school, work, kids' activities—working?
22. Is the climate OK?

23. Type of accommodation, house, apartment, all right?

And that, ladies and gentlemen, is the *famous one-hun*. For now. Clearly this list will evolve! He declared. We *will* press on, he threatened.

Yikes! It was hard to imagine *more*.

Seeing Triple

So now when we step back and look at our lives, when we analyze our life's circumstances, when we take stock, we can recognize that we not only need to look at both our work and non-work lives, but we need also to look at our working life two different ways. We need to consider our job *context* as well as our job *content*.

Doing so, we end up seeing triple, seeing in three dimensions, seeing in 3D! We see job content, job context and life context. It allows us to not only see the meal, but we see *every* ingredient in it.

By raising to the level of consciousness these one hundred ingredients, we are in a far better position to fine-tune our circumstances, to improve our daily menu.

We become Master Chefs!

He then took *his* chef's hat off and wiped his brow.

I know that took a long time he said, but knowing this I think is worth it. Check that, he said. Knowing this *I know*, is worth it.

Knowing this changed my life!, he revealed.

And it changed my life, too.

the mover

G reat job, he said, now let's put what we know about all of these ingredients to work!

He's now dressed up just like the mover guy.

Where's the piano? he asked, I like to get that first. It helps me get warmed up!

Where are we headed this time?

Turns out he was going to help us relocate from *Is*, in the emotional state of Intensity to the little town of *Wannabe*, located in the great emotional state of *Easygoing*.

Only if we wanted to, of course, he said.

We were game.

Counselor figured there were two emotional states on the map. Both at the extremes of the well-being landscape. And both states, he reported, he had visited.

Both states, Counselor?

Yup, I've seen 'em both. First hand! Thing is though, we tend not to stay in either state real long, he slanged.

The one state is called *Intensity*. The other is called

Easygoing. And I assure you, I enjoyed my stay at *Easygoing* a lot more than my stay at *Intensity*.

You may have visited both states yourself, he continued. We visit the emotional state of *Intensity* when our ingredients are out of whack. We visit *Easygoing* when our ingredients are *configured* just right. But because we are constantly trying to make headway, trying to improve, because *there* doesn't stay *there* very long, we tend not to stay in *Easygoing* long either.

We're quick to get out of *Intensity* and by the time we catch our breath in *Easygoing*, our definition of what is possible has shifted out, and so to with it does the location of *Easygoing* on the map.

This couldn't be better though, he assured us, 'cause *that's* what keeps us growing. This need to grow is positive, something to anticipate and something to look forward to.

Easygoing is where we catch our breath, take some time to enjoy what we have accomplished and re-energize as we continue our journey. It is where we rest as we reconfigure what *could* be.

How Do We Know When We Are Visiting The State of Intensity?

So how will we know when things are out of whack? How will we know when we are in *Intensity*?

By:

What We Do

- we make our dog nervous when we walk by, the dog knows
- we assume a zombie-like trance to tolerate perceived indignities

---

- we become *not fun* to be around
- we become hard to get along with
- we can't even get along with ourselves
- we begin abdicating responsibility
- we waste time thinking and talking negatively about people
- we waste money
- we waste emotion
- we do things that are not positive role modeling behaviours for our children
- we develop a *game face* to survive
- we speak in a monotone
- our focus turns to surviving, getting by, somehow *getting through this* as opposed to accomplishing something
- we *look out for* as opposed to *look forward to*
- we are critical and unaccepting
- we make mistakes; we dig holes for ourselves; we compound the bad
- we catch ourselves saying *what else can go wrong?*
- we say *why me?*

How We Feel

- we feel powerless and hopeless
- our self respect and sense of personal dignity begin to erode
- we are constantly tired because we are making poorer and poorer lifestyle choices
- we begin to conclude that *none of this* is our doing and that it is out of our hands
- Fridays are acceptable, Saturdays are tolerable, occasionally fun, but Sundays are terror because Mondays follow

- our guts churn
- we feel regret because we know our families know we are suffering

How We Know When We Are Visiting the State of Easygoing

And how will we know when we are headed straight for *Easygoing*?

By:

What We Do

- we catch ourselves saying what else can go right and why *not* me?
- we cause the dog's tail to wag just by walking by, the dog knows
- we take more things in stride
- we are more accepting, giving and outward
- we take better care of ourselves
- our voices become animated
- we are more and better able to take care of, and attend to others; we have more to give
- we have more energy than we know what to do with because we are making wiser lifestyle choices
- we have our finances under control
- we waste little or no time worrying or thinking negatively about others
- we may even be a *hoot* to be around, or at least more of a *hoot* than we were
- our kids are learning good things from us just by watching how we behave, our approach to things and the decisions we make—we become positive role models for them

- instead of being an emotional drain for our family we turn into a source of energy
- we take our *game face* off and become genuine
- we build momentum; good things multiply
- we develop compound interests and our interest in life compounds

How We Feel

- we have a positive outlook and are constantly scanning for opportunities
- we feel more in control of our own situations
- we have more self-respect and a greater sense of personal dignity
- water slides off a duck's back, and we, for the first time ever, are the duck
- we don't mind *as much* when people cut in front of us on the highway—*as much*, he stressed
- we're more relaxed
- we *look forward to* as opposed to *look out for*
- we have a sense of self-determination and self-directedness. We are self-assured
- Fridays are great days to try to get appointments for the following week, Saturdays are wonderful days for the family, and Sundays are peaceful times to reflect and prepare

That said, how do we make the trip from *one state* to another? Well, the reality is that most of us don't have *that* far to travel. And most of us are intuitively making that trip everyday, anyway.

However, he said, I do have a few ideas on how to *help you* move your *is* a little closer to your *would like to be.*

We were eager to listen.

The distance between *Is* and *Wannabe* was right around thirteen miles. He even showed us on a map he'd made up.

And Counselor was going to be the guy who would help us make the move, if we wanted to. He was going to pack us up and move us. And show us the thirteen mile-markers along the way. Kilometers for the *kids*, he conceded.

Before we make the move, though, there are a few things we ought to pack with us, he said, a few ways we might want to consider looking at things to help us make the trip.

It involves steeling our resolve and taking charge. But it also involves cutting ourselves some slack.

Movin' From Is to Wannabe

We must first recognize, he suggested, not for the first nor for the last time that day, that we all have choices. Many people will help with our efforts. But it has been my experience, he said, that *if it is to be, it is up to me.* It is up to *us* to initiate.

And the changes we may need to make? They will, in all likelihood, center around the one hundred ingredients we just introduced. And the range of choices around each of the ingredients, by way of reminder, are:

Choice One

We can change what we can of the ingredient we identify needs changing, or

Choice Two

We can change how we feel about or cope with that specific ingredient, or

Choice Three

We can do both; we can make changes to the extent that we can to that ingredient *and* we can change how we feel about/cope with that specific ingredient at the same time. The double-barreled approach.

Counselor went on to make two more points before he gave us his *Roadmap to Easygoin.*

And Versus Or

A favourite word of mine, as you may know by now, is the word *and*, he began.

Why?, he continued...

Because replacing the word *or* with the word *and* in our vocabulary and in the way we look at things opens up an entire array of possibilities. When a decision has to be made that involves choices, we almost always say we can do this *or* we can do that. The word *and* changes all of that!

The word *or* is limiting. The word *and* is boundless, he said as he gathered momentum.

The tyranny (Definition: cruel and unjust use of power, the ruling with no leniency) of the *OR* gives way to the liberty of the *AND*, he shot across the bow as he crescendoed, an imaginary sword thrust skyward in his left hand, his popgun wielding right hand now clenched steadfastly over his heart.

When an *either-or* question comes up in our lives then,

we must *at least* consider saying *yes*, he pleaded. Why can't I do both or at least part of both?

He then gave us some examples:

- Should I go to work full time or finish my degree? Absolutely I should! I can go to school part-time *while* I work full-time. It will take all kinds of patience from my family, and me, and all kinds of effort and a little more time, but the point is I *can* do both.

- Should we fix the patio or golf? Yes. We just get up earlier so we can finish the patio and then hit the links.

- Should we visit your parents or mine at Christmas? The answer is yes! We'll visit one set Christmas Eve and have Christmas Dinner with the other. It might be a little nuts and require lots of give and take but our parents are irreplaceable. He paused for just a moment thinking back... We owe them a debt of gratitude, he said solemnly, once again getting lost in thought...

- Should we do this or should we do that? Without a doubt we should!, the implication left to dangle...

Replace I will do this *or* I will do that, with I can do this *and* I can do that. Be creative. Where there is a will there is a way. Where there is an *or*, there can be an *and*!

It is just how we look at things, he said.

Try it, it works, he enthused. We might not end up being able to do all of one or the other, but we can most times end up doing some of what we need to do of both. It is an incredible way of looking at things. And one he assured us that will pay off.

Time Well Spent

And second, to those of us who are feeling guilty for

all of this personal reflection, let me assure you, this time is well spent. Know that this effort will pay off for everyone. The happier and more at peace we are, the more able we are to attend to the Pomtgrs of others; the better positioned we are to lend an ear when somebody else needs it. Which, he observed, is a very generous thing!

I encourage you not to begrudge the time you spend *getting you right*; looking at the ingredients that make up your recipe, he said. Because *getting you right*:

- pays handsome dividends to those you care most about and who care most about you
- allows you to better attend to those you love
- improves *their* world dramatically

At least that has been my experience, he said.

Roadmap From Is, Intensity to Wannabe, Easygoing

We were in the moving van now and he was driving... Scary.

Big picture? The trip from *Is* to *Wannabe* requires that we align our realities to what we know works for us in terms of the *famous one-hun*. That, he said, in a nutshell, is the big picture. Let me now provide some detail. Let me drive you past the mile-markers.

And with that, he checked both mirrors and put 'er into gear....

Mile-Marker One—Isolate and Consider Each One of the One Hundred Ingredients

Look at each *ingredient*. One at a time.

Every one?

Yup, every one! he said.

Mile-Marker Two—Identify Which Ingredients Deserve Your Attention

As you look at each ingredient, determine whether or not it is one that affects you by asking yourself:

- Does it catch my interest?
- Is this ingredient something that affects me or is it something I can just let be?
- Is this *ingredient* an energizer?
- Is it neutral with little to no effect on how I'm feeling? or,
- Is it a drainer, something I need to deal with?

We should concentrate on the biggest ones first. Look for the specific *ingredients* that are *costing* us the most wasted time and misspent emotion. And look for the ones that are *generating* the most positive energy and *adding* the most to our overall well-being.

Why? Because as we fine-tune our recipe going forward, we want to *keep what is working* and *address what is not*. Hold constant what works while we adjust what does not. I need to change/fix/finetune *this*, while I hold on to *that*.

When looking at *drainers* in particular he said, we really need to be honest with ourselves. We need to chase down the *real* problem. The crux of this exercise is to make sure that we come out of it making a proper diagnosis.

Is it the drainers themselves, is it how we are looking at them, or is it both? he challenged, never letting up.

Don't like fixing the wrong problem, he said.

Mile-Marker Three—Look For Patterns

Look for patterns in your life to help lock in on the

this's and the *that's*. To start seeing the types of job content, job context and life content ingredients that consistently work for you and to lock in on the ingredients that rub us the wrong way. To begin to isolate with laser-like precision the energizers and to similarly isolate those that are the stones in our shoes.

You will then start to realize that there are very specific, very consistent ingredients that are energizing, positive and constructive for you. Similarly, you may begin to recognize that there are dimensions/ingredients in the way we have configured our life's circumstances, that are consistently draining, negative and destructive.

Again, what can energize one person though can drain another. So this then is very much an individual exercise.

To complete this exercise, he continued, we can look at various time periods in our lives and take a 3D snapshot. We can even look at the lives of others through this 3D filter (their jobs, their work settings and their home life) to *distill up* the specific job content, job context and life contexts dimensions that we think would be ideal for us. We can undertake this exercise to *distill up* the *"us-specific"* patterns of likes and dislikes in each area of the three slices.

Through this exercise (using Appendices One through Five), you will start to unearth or discover the types of job content, job context and life context circumstances that are best for you. And you will do so in inexorable detail.

Inexorable?

Sorry, couldn't help myself, he said.

But the more detail, the better, he pulled, borderline extracting.

Here are some examples:

- I am always most happy when I am doing x type of work (x coming from our job content list)
- I find I am always most productive in a work setting that includes a, b and c, but that definitely excludes x, y and z. (a,b,c, x, y, and z being plucked from the job context dimensions we laid out)
- I prefer a work space that has....
- I most enjoy it when I have this much and type of people contact...
- Life seems right when my home life includes this amount of exercise and that amount of studies
- I am always happiest when I live within x miles of my extended family. And x can be point five, five, or five hundred. It all depends on the individual

And this pattern/preference identification exercise, to be most productive, needs to be extremely specific, he *re-reiterated*:

- I really prefer the type of schedule that allows me to....
- I have always done well when I have used the following skills...
- I have always been brutal when I have had to do these types of jobs...
- I truly have a knack for...
- I do my best work when I....
- I am most at peace when I....
- My work setting should include...
- I have worked best with this type of leadership...
- At home, things work best when...
- I felt best when my health and lifestyle habits included...

Look at past life experiences and time periods and

distill it up:

- look at when you were the happiest and distill up the ingredients that worked
- look at when you were most miserable to isolate the causes
- look at others you know and look at what you like about their lifestyle and their approach to life and what of that you would like to incorporate into yours.

What do you know about you that would help you configure a more peaceful and productive existence? What should you get rid of? What should you keep? What should you fine-tune?

Mile-Marker Four—Create A Custom Fit

The upshot, the target for all of this, he said, is to align to the extent that we can, each dimension of our life, each of the one-hun, with what we know works for us. We all have to work. And every job has a setting in which it is performed. And we all need to live somewhere, he said.

Revelation after revelation, he kidded himself.

But that *that* is our reality, he continued, why not try to understand ourselves better so as to customize our life's circumstances more closely to what we know works? We intuitively do this anyway. *Now we can consciously do it.*

We can consciously navigate the journey from *Is* to *Wannabe*, he reassured as he tipped his Mover's cap.

If you look at it, it is no different than custom making a suit or getting a pair of shoes that fit.

Take your measurements. Find out what type of job content, job context and life context conditions are best for you. Know yourself, and then sew the outfit; the job content, the job setting and the life setting that works for you. The one that will be a custom fit for you.

Remember a custom suit fits better than one off the rack. And also remember that a shoe that doesn't fit causes blisters. And while we can tolerate anything for a while, if the shoe is drastically wrong-sized, it can cause permanent damage, leaving a scar.

To deal properly with all of this, we can use a "way of looking at things tape measure" to create the custom fit.

An Awful Look

It was at this point that our dear Counselor almost exploded with frustration. He didn't look good.

Problem, Counselor?

There is.

What is it?

I'm consternated.

That doesn't sound good.

It's not. Here is the issue...

I only have one day with you and there is so much I need you to know! And I have a *file* that I wish to download to your WP, but it will take too long to do it here and now! I must therefore introduce you to it here, and then provide you with the links to *download* it into your WP when you get home. Will that be acceptable?

That will be fine, we said, willing to agree to anything to get his heart rate down.

I thank you, he said, the normal colour returning to his face.

Here then is the overview, the abbreviated version of what I want you to know and then how you can chase down additional detail.

There is a concept called *type technology,* first developed by Carl Jung, that helps us understand why we do the things we do. It helps us more readily recognize patterns in our behaviour. It helps us more quickly recognize patterns in what works for us and what doesn't, in all aspects of our lives. Type technology helps us understand why we do what we do and why others do what they do.

This technology helps us custom fit our job content, job context and life context. It helps us take our measurements so we can custom fit. It helps take away much of the guess work, the trial and error. Not all of it, but some of it.

I have used it for career planning, my own, he said, relationship building, team building, business building, for self and other understanding and for self and other acceptance.

Suffice it to say that I have leaned on this filter through which we can view things.

This technology or understanding will help you to put labels on how you feel and perhaps help explain:
- why Spock was Spocklike and why Scotty was Scotty
- why some prefer social work while others appear to be born for sales
- why some people literally *need* to be with people while others prefer time alone
- why some people seem to have a knack for numbers while others seem to sense feelings that others can't begin to
- why some people are always inclined to want to paint rooms white (they live in the future and are concerned about resale) while others prefer bright colours (who cares about resale?—let's go for it *now*)

- why some people rely on the facts when making up their minds while others seem to use their guts
- why some people work best in groups while others prefer to work alone
- why some people love to schedule their days minute by minute, while others prefer to simply let things happen
- why some people inevitably clash
- how to help them avoid this
- why we might rub some people the wrong way
- why some teams fail
- why the same work setting can be perfect for one but completely counterproductive for another
- why the same person can affect one person one way and another person in a completely different way
- why some people use a plumb bob when they wallpaper and some just *eyeball* it
- why some people live in the future and are therefore, best in certain jobs, and while others live in the here and now, and are better at other jobs
- why some people use their head more than their heart, while others use their heart more than their head when they make decisions
- why and how what we, and others, do is not all that random
- why and how we write, speak, act, communicate and even decorate our surroundings is telling, and sometimes even predictable
- how the type of jobs we do and setting we prefer can be customized according to *type* (how we get energized, the type of information we notice most readily, how we decide things and whether we prefer a structured day or

one that allows flexibility)

It is technology that will help us more formally *take our measurements*; understand what fits and what doesn't, as we try to customize our life's fit. This way of looking at things, this lens, helps us get to know ourselves far more quickly than having to learn by experience what works for us.

It helps us understand and accept ourselves and understand and accept others. And frankly, the self understanding that we gain from knowing this technology helps us get along with others and ourselves far better.

We cut ourselves and others more slack because we can now more easily sense when we are *doing it* again, or *overdoing* it again. It also helps us understand where our strengths lie, and areas that do not come to us as naturally, which in turn can help us make more informed choices; about our careers, how we perceive people and how we behave.

This technology helps demystify/unbundle/provide us with a filter through which to view how and why we do what we do, and how and why others do what they do. When combined with our understanding of the *famous one-hun*, this knowledge creates a *formidable arsenal of self-understanding*; one that I believe puts us in a position to make far more informed decisions.

I have used this technology, he said, to self monitor and appreciate the differences in people. We can use it to see where our strengths lie and to see where we need to spend extra time.

My purpose today, he said, is to serve as your gateway to this knowledge. This knowledge is of value whether you are a student or a senior, a career planner or someone wishing to understand a relationship better. It is simply a way of looking at things that helps. I wish only to light a fire, to sufficiently whet your appetite so that you will be compelled to chase this knowledge down once we are done here.

You will recall our conversation about the three nines and two tens; the need to know what we have in our hand and which game is best for us? We can either do it by trial and error, intuitively, or we can actively deploy additional self-understanding tools to help us get to know us better. Physicians use thermometers and X-rays to diagnose, tailors use tape measures. And so, too, are there tools to help *us* get to know *us* better.

Trial and error is necessary but the use of more formal tools can accelerate our progress. My recommendation then is to say *yes* to all of these approaches. We then dramatically reduce the distance between *Intensity* and *Easygoing*. I, therefore, recommend a sidetrip to the local college or university, bookstore or Website to chase down the following related self-understanding tools to help speed up the trip:

- Please Understand Me—a book by Paul Keirsey and Marilyn Bates
- Do What You Are—a book by Paul Tieger and Barbara Barron-Tieger
- http://www.cpp-db.com—a web-site linking you to the Myers-Briggs Type Indicator®, an instrument of self-understanding that is globally recognized and also grows out of Jung's work.

Mile-Marker Five—Evolve Your Reality To Align With Your Likes and Your Good Ats

The next step, he said involves making change;

emphasizing the energizers and managing the drainers. Much more easily said than done, but altogether doable, he assured us.

I invite you to take the rest of your life for this task, he said, not being facetious. But celebrate each step along the way. Each ingredient fine-tuned adds tremendously to the richness of our existence here. Removing even the smallest of pebbles from our shoe makes the journey that much more comfortable and allows us to go that much further.

Mile-Marker Six—Look At Job Content First

Go right back to the job content ingredients. Determine the *alignment* with your *preferences*. Are there skills you are using that aren't a strength? Are there strengths that you have that *aren't* being used? Can you evolve or rearrange your present job duties to include the strengths and play down the weaknesses?

Look at jobs you've had in the past. Use the Worksheets I have provided, (Appendices) he encouraged us.. Look at jobs that others have. What do you know you are good at and like? What do you know you need to play down or get rid of.

Big job or little job here? Major overhaul or simply fine-tune? Only you can know, he said.

Mile-Marker Seven—Now Look At Job Context

Look carefully at every one of the job context ingredients. Which ones drive you nuts? Which are only minor irritants? Which ones energize? What action steps can you take to either:

- change/modify/fine tune that contextual dimension – do what can you to change the situation
- change how you react to that dimension affect you
- do both?

Mile-Marker Eight—And Then Look At Life Context Dimensions

This for many is the most important part.

Look at each of these to unearth those ingredients that are aligned and those that need your attention. This might mean dropping some things and adding others. Analyze how you are using your time and how you are using your mind. You will be amazed at what you discover, he foretold.

Mile-Marker Nine—Create Action Steps to Close the Gap Between Is and Wannabe

Once we have identified the areas that need adjustment; those ingredients in the recipe that need to be added, deleted or just fine-tuned a little, we can then start effecting change.

Begin with small steps and then work your way along:
- explore your alternatives for making change, different ways of coming at it. Be creative. Brainstorm. List *all* of the possibilities. Don't reject anything outright until you have worked through all of the possible angles. That includes how you are perceiving or reacting to each ingredient.
- objectively assess the most likely consequences of making those changes
- make the changes

Mile-Marker Ten—Recognize the Rubik's Cube Effect

If you have ever tried to align a Rubik's Cube, you know that whenever you adjust one row or column, it affects all of the other rows and columns. Just when we have one row all lined up, we have to change it to get the other row lined up. As with the Rubik's Cube though, Counselor assured us that it is possible to get all of our rows and columns lined up. It is possible to configure our job content, job context and life context *just so*. It just takes some time and some effort. It also takes *knowing* that we have to *manage all three* of our life's dimensions, each one of the *famous one-hun*, to get it just right.

Mile-Marker Eleven—Pack a Lunch...and a Dinner

Be patient, he stressed again, the trip may be short but it usually takes time. It will take time to understand our needs and then to gravitate or evolve our circumstances, to fine-tune the ingredients. Sometimes we don't even know what type of job or job setting we prefer until we have had several years of experience. It takes time to learn what cards we have been dealt and what game is our best!

My trip has taken well over seventy years, he smiled, and I *still* have a ways to go!

Experiencing things takes time. That's why he suggested packing a lunch *and* dinner.

The other reason to pack well is the nature of the road. The trip from *Intensity* over to *Easygoing* is not always smooth. There may be detours and roadblocks and potholes as well. In some instances we'll simply need to refuel.

But if we keep our eye on the road, remain in gear, and be a little more than patient, we can usually arrive.

And it is the journey, as much as the arriving, that makes the trip fun!

And it was at this point that he held up his map.

Lookeee here, he screeched in his best southern drawl...

Is, by my way of thinkin' and accordin' to this map, *is* always closer to *could be* than it is to *was*.

We just smiled. What else could we do?

Trapeze Act

He finished this point up by acknowledging what some of us were thinking. This trip may be a family trip and in that case requires superhuman coordination. To properly configure each of our family members' *famous one-huns*, at the same time, requires the kind of:

- constant communication
- trust
- honesty
- commitment
- courage
- flexibility
- sacrifice
- support
- patience
- give and take

found typically only in circus trapeze acts. To synchronize and coordinate multiple careers and all family member dreams at the same time is obviously a challenge.

But he also knew that we knew that our families were up to the task. Because if the truth be known, our families would have to have been master jugglers just to rearrange schedules long enough to get us here to meet with our Counselor in the first place!

So a toast to our families?

We all clinked our juice.

Just Knowing Helps

He also suggested that *just knowing* helps.

Just knowing *where* we want to go and unearthing what has to be dealt with, makes it easier to be where we are at. We feel peace and remarkable calm when we know our direction, even if we haven't begun our journey yet. A sense of peace sets in when we resolve where we wish to head. Even if we haven't started the trip and even if the way isn't clear.

It is the *not knowing*—not knowing where we are headed—that can be the most frustrating and leave us feeling most out of control, he noted, having lived it.

It is the peace of mind that comes from this personal discovery that eases the tension and yields the type of contentment that most of us seek.

Knowing *where* we want to go—job content, job context and life context—makes the how we're going to get there far, far easier. It lets us chart the course and plot the journey in a more controlled and measured manner. It is hard to get *there* when *there* isn't clear.

It also became clear at about this time in the session that he was handing *us* the keys. Only you know your *Is* and only you know your *Wannabe*. Equipped with this road map, we were now in control. We could now find our own way to *Wannabe*. We could effect change, make the journey, close the gap at our own pace.

Being clearer on the process, we could take this trip, make the changes we wish, at a less disruptive, more considerate and more constructive pace for all concerned. Instead of breaking the speed limit and possibly getting lost along the way, we could now more likely keep an eye on the map and the speed limit, and more fully enjoy the ride.

He made it clear though, that other tools would help with the trip.

Mile-Marker Twelve—Use Other Tools

You can't build a house equipped with just a hammer, he analaphored.

There are other tools to help us as we make this trip:

- use your *adult* to conduct the analysis, to evaluate the likely consequences of what you are considering and to generate your action plan
- use your *internal locus of control* to take charge of your situation
- make the trip more quickly by *Pracellerating*
- strap on your *Seat belt*
- check your *Arsenal*

With all due respect Sir, what the...

I haven't introduced all of these tools yet? he wisecracked.

Well I guess you'll have to stay for the whole day, sticking his hooks in, hoping no one would leave early.

He then wrapped it up...

Mile-Marker Thirteen—Get Started/Get Some Traction

Effecting positive personal change feeds on itself. So just get started, he encouraged. Do something, even if it *seems* very small.

Once we make one change, the next change comes more easily, which in turn makes making subsequent changes come even easier.

A wheel once in motion tends to *stay* in motion, he Newtoned!

The trick though, he reinforced, is to *just get started*. One thing. Any thing. It's like getting traction. The wheels spin for a while but if we keep at it, and start slowly, our tires will get traction. And once we get traction and get going, we can move even faster.

These words gushed from a guy who had wheeled our moving van and had then given us the keys.

We knew it was our job now to chart own course to *Easygoing*.

But it was nice to have had him show us the way.

the driver's seat

A s you have just experienced, being a passenger is OK, but it can also be frustrating. Not that I was all that bad behind the wheel, I hope, he said. But when you want to get somewhere and someone else is driving, or you *feel* that some*thing* else is driving, it can get well past frustrating.

The point is, it is hard to get to where we want to go when we feel that we are not in control. And being more in control of our own destiny, being in the driver's seat, is what most of us prefer. It is where we are most at peace.

Agreed.

This next Attitool then, the Driver's Seat, helps us learn how to go from feeling like a passenger to feeling more like we are the ones behind the wheel. We learn how to *take* charge and feel more in control. It helps us see a bit of what's going on *under the hood.* It highlights some of the *mechanics* of the different ways we can process things.

Not A Second Too Early

And *now* I suspect, is not a second too early to introduce you to this way of thinking, *especially* after all of this talk about making changes in our lives.

True?

More true than he knew.

Locus Of Control

I would like to introduce you to a personality dimension that I briefly mentioned earlier. It is one that already exists as a feature of our WorldProcessor, Counselor began. It is a significant part of the filtering process we use to make sense of our life's circumstances or events. It is the filter we use to decide whether we feel we are in charge of our life's events and outcomes, or whether we feel that what happens to us is a twist of fate or luck.

It is a measure of our perspective on control. This personality dimension is a meaningful part of our perceptual filter, our WorldProcessor. This filter is activated all the time, processing data about what is happening around us; sending us messages and telling us how to interpret events.

The name of this feature or component, this dimension of each of our personalities, is Locus of Control. Locus (or place) of Control is the extent to which we believe we control the events in our lives. It is a continuum, somewhere along which our beliefs reside.

Julian Rotter, a social psychologist in the mid-1960's, determined that people could be placed along a continuum based on how much they believed they controlled their life's happenings and the extent to which they felt luck or fate controlled these occurrences. This lens on how we process life's events is a measure of the extent to which we believe that what happens to us is under our control or a result of external forces.

And this *way of thinking*, this *I caused that to happen* versus *that was out of my hands* set of options, is part of our make-up, a feature of our existing WorldProcessor, and a changeable part at that.

This is a classic Attitool because it is one of the ways we can and do view and process the world. It is already a part of our WorldProcessor. It runs constantly, up until now, largely unnoticed but impacting heavily on how we process events, how we decide to react to these events and then ultimately, on how we feel.

As we raise this personality dimension to the level of consciousness, we will discover how significant an effect locus of control has on our outlook; how optimistic or pessimistic we feel, how much hope we have or how hopeless we may feel.

Things are sometimes worse for folks, worse for us; frankly, they were worst for me, Counselor confessed, when I felt out of control. Conversely, things have never been better since *learning* to better manage this very important way of looking at things.

I guess you could say, I Re-Attitooled, he told us.

Let's continue, he said... Here are the two dimensions of the locus of control scale:

Internals

At one end of the scale are internals. Internals have decided or learned to believe that their fate is largely in their own hands. They believe that what happens to them in the world, whether they *get ahead* (or not) make friends (or not), have things go their own way (or not), is largely a result of their own doing. They carry with them an outlook that is very much an *if it is to be, it is up to me* way of viewing things and they tend to act and feel according to those beliefs.

Bottom line? Internals feel *in control*. They feel they are in the Driver's Seat. They feel they control events around them and can strongly influence what happens. They tend to be optimistic and hopeful. They take charge to the extent that they can of the events that affect them.

Externals

At the other end of the scale are externals. Externals have learned or decided to believe that their fate is determined largely by good and/or bad luck. Their mindset is *my fate is out my hands* or *I can't do anything about this*. Externals believe that their fate; what they have, what happens to them; is a function of what others do or have done. It is a function of luck.

They feel like the ball in someone else's Ping Pong game, and they too, tend to act according to those beliefs; allowing events to unfold.

Bottom line? Externals believe they do not control events around them. They feel like *stuff* is just happening and there is little, if anything, they can do to change events or their outcome. They feel less hopeful and less optimistic.

Both of these ways of looking at things can emerge as a dominant lens or perspective on the way we view life.

How We Get There

Our life's experiences, what we believe to be true, what we have seen others close to us experience, all combine to make up the lines of code that is the Locus of Control feature or component of our WorldProcessor. And while most of us are somewhere in-between the extremes of internal and external, we can all nevertheless see the impact on our well-being of being either predominantly one way or the other. We make decisions about how to act, how to feel and how to behave based on those beliefs, that is, based on what our current Locus of Control program is telling us.

So it makes sense then to do a WorldProcessor bug check to see if what we currently have running is what we *want* to have running. And if it isn't, do a little program upgrade to switch a little away from external beliefs over to internal.

Counselor assured us that this was doable. When he discovered this feature of *his* WP, he went in and did a little reprogramming. Sure enough he said, he was able to reprogram away from feeling like a passenger, feeling external, when it came to making things happen in his life, to feeling more like he was in the driver's seat, feeling more internal.

And he was certain that if *he* could do it, so could we!

Examples

Here is an example of the conversation we can have with *our voice inside* that will give us a feel for how our *Locus of Control* way of looking at things operates within our WP; and in turn how it can affect how we decide to act, react or behave.

I didn't get the promotion. Boss's fault or mine? An external response might be to say that it was the boss's fault because he just wanted somebody with this degree /designation or someone who could work those types of hours. Well I don't have that degree nor can I work those types of hours, so the outcome is out of my hands.

An internal response on the other hand might be, I could have at least competed more effectively for that job, if not gotten it, had I chosen to take the extra courses for that designation and chosen to work those hours.

So that I did not receive that promotion was at a minimum, partially my doing and to some extent, a matter of choice. I am therefore somewhat accountable for the outcome.

Or I *did* get the promotion because I *chose* to take extra courses and chose to rearrange my schedule. These thoughts too are *internal* beliefs at work.

The outcomes we look at can either be positive or negative; I get the promotion or I don't get the promotion. It is *how* we look at the outcomes that gives us insight into whether we hold primarily internal beliefs (Yeah, it did or did not work out, but at least it was my own doing) or external beliefs (Yeah, I got that promotion but I'll be darned if I know why).

Another Example

I received a poor grade on my assignment because I missed a class. There could be two distinct views of the same event, depending on one's perspective, depending on one's Locus of Control.

The external perspective goes this way. I *had* to miss the class where the teacher gave details about the assignment because I *had* to go to a meeting. So, basically my mark can't be all my fault (be it good or bad). An internal perspective goes like this: I am responsible for that lower mark because I made an active choice. I chose to go to the meeting and the consequence was that the assignment was discussed without me knowing about it, and without me following up with the Professor. I did not get the information I needed to get the mark I wanted. I don't like the outcome but I know I am accountable for that decision. I therefore remain in charge of my marks, good or bad.

Active choices lead to consequences.

Locus of Control rides on *who* we believe is ultimately accountable, the event or us.

Again, reality and accountability almost always lie somewhere inside the extremes but these scenarios provide some insight into the *two ways* of viewing situations.

Self-optometrization opportunity, someone piped up?

Exactly, he confirmed.

While the first thing we pick up is that it is probably not wise to be an extreme internal or an extreme external, we also pick up that by moving to a more internal perspective, we can begin to feel more in control of our own destiny, more optimistic and more hopeful.

Transitioning to more internal beliefs, he said, is something we can learn. And because this lens is learned and evolves, it is also something that can be *unlearned* and then relearned; something that can be toned. It is like identifying a muscle set in our bodies and resolving to strengthen it.

Tangent Warning!

Like my *abs*, he said. We almost knew *this* was coming.

You know I've been working out, he advised us.

He was now clearly headed off on one of his *way too much detail* tangents, so we tuned him back in before he hit the deck. He was threatening to do sit-ups. We weren't ready for that!

He *lost it*, only occasionally.

Ah yes, my apologies, he said. Clearing his throat, and a little embarrassed, he promptly pressed on. He did say, though, that he was up to twenty *crunches* with no stopping!

He had accomplished his objective, though. Not once did he miss an opportunity to even subtly plant in our minds visions of what is possible. Seventy-five years old? Twenty sit-ups? What then, is possible for us, not just in terms of our health but in every aspect of our lives? He consciously tried to get at our subconscious. He wanted to help us stretch, grow and discover new ways of appreciating the *limitlessness* of our potential, *shattering* our perspective of what is possible, to *expand* what we once thought we were capable of. We later learned that he actually had another tool to help us do just that; the Pracellerator.

Mission accomplished, he returned to giving us tools to empower us, to help us feel more in control of our own destiny.

How Do We Know When We Are Acting According To External Beliefs?

- when we accept *que sera sera* as the norm
- when we say we had no choice...it was completely out

of our hands
- when we feel it is up to others more than us
- when we feel it is caused by others more than us
- when we feel there are few things we can do to fix it
- when we lay blame
- when we react
- when we look to others
- when we tell ourselves *I am a victim of circumstance* more than *I am the author of my own destiny*
- when we say *you make me feel* more than *I make feel*

How Will We Know When We Are Acting Internally?

- when we proact instead of react
- when we begin to believe *if it is to be, it is up to me*
- when we realize we always have choices. They may not always be pretty but in principle we always have choices
- when we feel it is up to us more than others
- when we feel it is created or caused more by us than others
- when we feel there are many things we can do to fix it
- when we assume responsibility
- when we tell ourselves *I am the author of my own destiny* more than *I am the victim of circumstance*
- when we say *I make me feel* more than *you make me feel*
- when we accept that when we *burn our backsides, we sit on the blister*

How we react to or prepare for any event is a choice.

How Do We Go From External Locus Of Control Beliefs To Internal?

Counselor reiterated that he felt that our Locus of Control perspective evolved. It was learned and therefore could be unlearned, reconfigured, and relearned. He felt this because he had done it himself!

It was simply a matter of knowing that we could look at events in one of two ways, internally or externally, and then *choose* which way to go. It was a matter of looking at things through a different lens. And convincing/teaching/retraining that voice inside to ask what of this situation can I control, influence and have an impact on, as opposed to having it say this is or was out of my hands.

That Voice Inside

Convince *that voice inside* that at least to some extent, in most cases *we* are in the Driver's Seat and can steer the outcome. Over time, as we realize we can have at least some impact, that we *do* have a say and that we *always* have choices, when we actually do have some wins, the need for convincing diminishes. That voice inside, the one we control with the Clicker, automatically begins asking *what part of this can we influence?* It gets reprogrammed. It experiences an upgrade.

This is just one way, he said, that we could retrain *that voice inside*. We train it to be an ally. We train it to be upbeat and ask what we can do, as opposed to reminding us of what we can't. We transform it from being a yappy *back seat driver* into being a trusted ally, providing valuable input and options instead of toxic mental waste.

We can reprogram it to look for the possibilities as

opposed to what's wrong, to look for what we can influence in the situation as opposed to what we can't. To see how much is in the glass as opposed to how little there is.

I believe that this journey, from external to internal, is not easy, he confessed. However, it can be the most worthwhile, personally empowering and rewarding journey some of us will ever take.

More internal Locus of Control beliefs serve as part of the fuel we need to help us make change.

So how do we fuel up? How do we get energized? How do we slide from the passenger's seat over to the driver's side?

Step One—Recognize that this Personality Dimension Exists

Knowing that this personality dimension exists is ninety percent of the battle. Now that we have raised these possible ways of looking at things to the level of consciousness, we can make active choices. Now that we know it's there, we can do something about it. Before it was just a vague feeling, something we only saw in results. Now we control it. We are no longer the passenger. We are now in the driver's seat, if we choose to be.

Knowing that we can choose which way to view the world and our life's circumstances gives us the license to grab the wheel. It does not mean that there will not be rough road ahead. There will be. But at least it will be by choice if we go *off road*. Because sometimes, that is a quicker way to get where we want to go.

We're Driving!

Step Two - Recognize That We Have Choices

Nobody forces us to do anything in life. We are one-hundred percent free to make choices and select from alternatives.

And while each alternative has consequences associated with it, as we have discussed before, the point is, we have choices. And the minute we cross that bridge of understanding, the more we are able to move from external to internal. The more apt we are to broaden our thinking and consider more alternatives.

Step Three—Feel Free to Stop At the Concession Stand

I know some of this must be tough to hear, he acknowledged. It is not an easy trip from external to internal. Particularly in some instances. It may also be thirsty work! We may therefore need to stop at a concession stand on the way through from external to internal. There may be occasions, even when we know the theory, when we feel completely out of control.

Circumstances may conspire against us to the point where we feel absolutely powerless. There may be situations that come up that leave us feeling gut-twisting, fist-slamming, drawer-hoisting mad because there is something that has happened, is happening or will happen that affects us directly that we feel we can't do a darn—that's as far as he would go—thing about!

And it is during these situations, right at that very moment he said, that we'll need to pull over and stop at the Concession Stand. We may need to concede/acknowledge, at that point, how awfully frustrating this situation is. How maddening, how *angsting* it is. Because it is that, and sometimes even more than that. And we may *need* to acknowledge *that* before we can successfully move, a pause at this Concession Stand may be necessary. This is where we can pick up a Venting Licence, he told us, but more on that later as well.

He was *right* though. What we were talking about was our natural human capacity to dust ourselves off and get back in the race. Even though we have this Locus of Control capacity, we may still occasionally run aground where we feel we are out of control. The thinking though is that knowing that this way of looking at things exists, maybe we can get back up a little quicker, slow down and arrest an emotional freefall.

Knowing that we have processes for wresting control, if not of the outcome, at least of how we deal with it, in fact slides us more to the driver's side. Perhaps not right away, but perhaps more quickly than before.

When we first learn to use this tool, our *is* still won't be our *could be*, he told us...

But it *will* be better than our *before*, we chimed in, having now committed his motto to memory.

Step Four—Look For Pieces

Granted I might not be able to control this situation *outright*, but *what of* it can I influence is how we begin to look at things. There must be something of this that I can control. If nothing more than *how I manage myself* while I *figure out how to manage this*!

And this is the key. Get a little win! Get part of it! Look for pieces of what you can do about it or how you will feel about it. After all, you own your outlook, he prodded.

What can I do to influence the outcome of this event? Perhaps I can't change the outcome or others' opinions overnight, but if I work methodically, perhaps I can influence the outcome over time. Perhaps if I present my position a little more this way or that, it might change things. Maybe if I view the situation through *their* eyes for awhile, I can start to see things that I am not seeing now. And if after all that, things still aren't right, then at least I will have given it every opportunity, and I am then free to choose how I proceed from here.

I may not control the outcome outright, but I can surely influence it and I can surely determine how I feel about it, and how I proceed!

I *can* look for pieces.

This Locus of Control feature also carries with it some degree of responsibility and action orientation. If we wish to take charge of our own destiny, it becomes incumbent upon us to seek out the facts, to learn what is going on; to not sit back.

Internal beliefs coincide with an action orientation; seeking out as opposed to waiting; acting as opposed to reacting; making things happen as opposed to letting things happen; making choices about how to feel; doing some digging before passing judgment.

Step Five—Talk It Out

Find a good listener, someone you trust, someone who doesn't judge, then *spill* your guts. Vent. Counselor could also get to the point with things, to the root of things.

Talk it out, he said. But take a pen, he insisted. As you talk it out, as you spill your guts, inevitably, possible ways of dealing with it, making it better, managing it, *come to you*. They emerge. They pop!

Thank your listener and *be there* to return the favour! It's amazing how family and friends help us wrest control of what once seemed out of our control, just by lending an ear. And we do the same for them.

It's even more amazing, he let dangle, how we help the most when we say the least...

Step Six—Catch Ourselves

Learn to recognize when this Locus of Control feature ought to be activated and learn when it is being activated using the *old*, external belief functionality. Learn to catch ourselves. Learn to recognize when we are *doing* it, acting externally, again. The key is to prevent an *it's out of my hands* go by unless we actively *choose* to let it do so.

Step Seven—Use This Lens To Analyze Past Events and To Provide Perspective

This is a terrific tool of analysis as well. We can use it as a lens to look back at past events and past outcomes. As I look back on past events, objectively, I can ask myself what aspects of those situations I could have controlled? Looking at how I reacted, could I have chosen to react any differently? Do I have choices now? Is there more that I can do now, knowing that I am, at a minimum, partially responsible for what happens to me here? He took a breath.

Using our Locus of Control filter to revisit our past actions and reactions to see if changing the lens we were using at the time has influenced the outcome is valuable. It points ups what we might be able to change in terms of our perspective or actions the next time something similar happens.

It distills up ways to look at things based on how we now view the past. We can't do anything about these things now, but we can most assuredly learn from them.

Some Questions

He then put up some questions we can teach our *voice inside* to ask, to help us be more in charge, to help us slide over to the Driver's Seat.

Sliding Over

- what part(s)/facets of this situation do I control?
- what part(s) of this situation can I influence?
- what part(s) of this situation, even after I wrack my brains, are clearly out of my hands?
- what are my alternate courses of action?
- what are the consequences associated with each alternative? Again, it is vital to explore *all* alternatives even if at first glance they appear to have no merit.
- who else should I involve?
- what advice do I need to go forward properly on this?
- when and how should I carry out the changes?
- what is the best thing/worst thing/most likely thing to happen (to me and those affected), if I implement what I am most strongly considering?
- is it now possible to shrink the list of things that are out of my control in this situation?

We can use this filter as a diagnostic tool, to make sense of what has happened in the past or use it to help us understand something that is happening right now. In addition, we can use it to project or predict what might happen if we choose a certain course of action.

The Wrap Around

Wrapping these questions around *any scenario* or situation helps slide us into the Driver's Seat as it relates to that situation. It inevitably yields an *I guess I control more of this than I thought* type of outcome.

The Wrap Around helps us deal with all kinds of issues.

- a change at work
- dealing with a coworker
- dealing with an ailing parent
- getting a degree
- getting our finances in order
- dealing with something frustrating that we didn't think we could impact
- planning a project
- helping us figure how to sprint from first base (where we are now) to second base (where we would like to be) without getting picked off (missing a mortgage payment). It affords us the luxury of being able to explore all alternative ways of going forward. If I do this, then that could happen. Could I, could we live with that? Yes? No? Next possible way of coming at this?...is the type of self-talk that grows out of this more empowered way of looking at things?

We discover that we have more control over situations, or at a minimum, have more control over how we feel about or react to situations, than we once thought.

It is a process that allows us to *chip away* at a problem

or a possibility, job content, job context or life context related, and helps us keep our sanity while we do it.

Examples:

To give us more of a feel for how it feels, here are some additional examples of *internal* thinking patterns in action:

- I can't control that I don't have a degree just yet, but I can control whether I take courses at night
- I can't control my boss's moods but I can control how I respond to them
- I can't do anything about how I handled my finances in the past, that is gone. However, I can determine how we go from here
- I can't control the coach's beliefs, but I can influence his opinion
- That those I looked up to did or did not do one thing, does not preclude me from doing or not doing another

This Attitool is a WorldProcessor *debugger* and a *personal capability unleasher*, he advertised. It is one that I encourage you to consider.

Step Eight—Enjoy the Ride

And finally, once we've done everything we can about a situation, asked every question of ourselves, explored every avenue, done whatever we could, it is then time to enjoy the ride!

Because, perhaps after all of our analysis, we may determine there is only a little we can do to alter the course of events or we may discover there are all kinds of things that we can do. The main point is that it is a terrific feeling to know that we have searched high and low and done all that we can. Our peace of mind relative to our grief and anxiety improves dramatically. Doing our best always does that! Breaking a sweat always feels good. Going that extra mile leaves our conscience clear.

Did I study as hard as I could? If yes, then sleep well.

Did I cover every angle in preparation for the presentation? If yes, then let the chips fall.

Did I do everything I could to see that the customer was well served? If yes, then stand easy.

Did I give it everything I had? Did I go the extra mile and then one? If yes, then clear your mind. Know that you have done all that could be done!

Did I put gas in the car, air in the tires and buckle up my Seat Belt? Did I do all I could to ensure a positive outcome? Did I, in so doing, place myself firmly in the Driver's Seat of my life? If yup, then kick back and enjoy the ride!

Was it perfect? Likely not. Was it the best we could do? Without question! That being the case, we should always rest well.

All we can do is the best we can do, he reassured us. And most times our best is *much* more than good enough!

the praccelerator

C lose your eyes!
Rustling noises...OK...Open'em!

His next outfit? A professional race car driver. Gloves. Helmet. Sponsors. Again. The whole deal. Authentic stuff too! Or so he told us....

Ladies and gentlemen, I am about to teach you how to Praccelerate, how to close the gap between our *is* and our *could be, faster* and better! The process has six stages and requires a pit crew and the sooner we get this process loaded into your WP, the quicker your trip to Easygoing!

Serious?

Serious.

Praccellerating—The Progress Accelerator

I first stumbled onto this process by accident and then formalized it so I could better *plan* my *luck*, he began, not missing a beat.

It is a process that allows us to effect significant positive personal change and go beyond what we once thought possible.

Pracellerating deals with our capacity and willingness to methodically discover what exceptional looks like, and then begin the process of replication. It stretches our capacity to *go beyond* where we are now, to reach new levels, by seeking out those who have done it and to then learning from them. We induce serendipity.

Those we seek out have already scaled the mountains that we want to climb. And many who have already done so will gladly reach down and pull us up, accelerating our progress, *if* we just ask! It is a process we can all use to close the gap between our *is's* and our desired *could be's*.

It is a process we can deploy to either create the circumstances to make change proactively or to take maximum advantage of a situation when it presents itself randomly.

Raising the Bar

This is a process we can use to accelerate the rate at which we make progress; Pracellerate; learn, accomplish things, and get results that we had not previously considered possible.

Let me walk you through the steps:

Step One—Identify What We Want to Do Better

Step One of the process involves identifying those areas in our lives where we would like to improve. We identify the mountains we want to climb. We think through what we would like to do or do better.

Many times though, these aren't mountains, they can just be everyday things we would like to do, or do better.

Counselor included a worksheet on this to help trigger our thinking. (Appendix Six).

Step Two—Locate Those Who Are Already Doing What We Want to Do

Step Two involves activating our Praccel-Scanners to locate Pracellerators.

Just one more time on that one, please?

The Praccel-Scanner is the feature of our WP we use to actively *seek out* those who have accomplished what we want to. By so doing, we learn what is possible, what great looks like, and how they made it so. By so doing, we stretch our definition of what is possible. We see what exceptional is and sometimes get an eye-opener.

He was cookin' now!

From building a deck to lowering our cholesterol; from improving our lighting to getting to VP; from building a business to curing a slice; from building a friendship to improving our outlook, we go to someone who did it and ask for their advice.

We find someone who did it, had it, earned it or built it and then ask'em how they did it, got it, earned it or built it!

Ideally we seek out people who have done exceptionally well at what we want to do; those who have been there and done that better than most who have been there and done that. We seek out the exceptions!

It All Starts with YaWanna

YaWanna build a deck, ya find somebody who built a *bute*. YaWanna do a degree part-time, ya find somebody who *aced* it. YaWanna have a certain type of career, ya get in touch with someone who's *nailing* it.

Step Three—Contact Them

Contact them! Get in touch with your Pracellerators: by telephone, e-mail, courier, pony express, lunch, breakfast, dinner, satellite, soup can and string, you name it! Somehow, get in touch.

Don't be shy. Tell them who you are and why you are getting in touch.

Most times they'll be flattered that you called. We're not going after rock stars here, we are approaching normal folks who have done what you and I consider to be really neat things; things we value and things we view as important to learn.

Step Four—Learn From Them

Step Four involves learning how they did it, learning what they know and applying it. Finding what went wrong and avoiding it. Finding out what went right and replicating it, emulating what worked and avoiding what didn't.

We don't need to reinvent the wheel. Most times, Pracellerators are more than willing, happy, maybe even flattered to share what they know with us.

But once you get their attention and permission, get the specifics and respect their time. Our senses must be set to *full receive* when we get our chance to meet with them. So be prepared! Get the details!

They will be very good at what they do so we must take full advantage of what they can teach us. Get the practical, ground level stuff.

Find out *exactly* what they did; how they did it; what time of day they worked on it; the stumbling blocks they encountered; what they would advise; how they measured what *good* was; who else you should speak to and what wasted their time. Find out what *they* thought a good day looked like, in terms of output and production, starting time and finishing time.

Ask them what you are forgetting and what you should forget.

Prepare for the meeting and ask them for details. Value their time. Have twenty detailed questions ready and written down before you meet. Get in. Take notes. Get out.

Step Five—Give It Time

Remember that our Pracellerators are already where we hope to be. So give it time and don't get flustered. We may be able to get where they are, but it will take time.

No matter what though, as a result of being exposed to them, our learning will undoubtedly be accelerated. Time will be saved, timelines drawn in, mistakes avoided and progress accelerated, the trip made quicker.

Our is may not immediately become our could be, but it will most likely end up being much better than our was, faster, as a result of Pracellerating.

Step Six—Follow Up and Thank Them

Step Six involves closing the loop. People love to help others. They also appreciate being appreciated. Thank them. Involve them. Keep them posted. Tell them exactly how and where their advice was used. And thank them again.

Learn What Is Possible

The key to Pracclerating is learning first hand, what is possible. It is seeking out those who have done what we want to do and then learning how they did it. Learning from folks not a whole lot different from you and me.

And why do this? Because once we see what possible, good, and exceptional really looks like, we realize how much of that we are actually capable of.

Let me say that again, he said, because it is central to our accomplishing what we want to accomplish. Ideally we *seek out* people who have done exceptionally well at what we are trying to do. We discover that they are not a whole lot different from you and me. Self-limiting chains then break free.

By so doing, we justifiably raise *our* bar and maybe reshape our perspective of what we are actually capable of. We poke through, we break through. The world of possibilities all of a sudden looks different.

Several of those *I didn't know I could do that* types of mental breakthroughs start to happen for us. And we thought that only happened when we were kids right, he kidded. But it can very definitely happen for us as adults, or so that was *his* experience.

By seeing what is actually being *accomplished* by others, we expand our definition of what is possible for us. We become inspired and justifiably energized.

We see what's possible and learn the nuts and bolts of how it was actually done. We can then determine what is a reasonable target for us.

We're not after perfection, but we can quickly move our *is* closer to our *Wannabe*!

Barrier Break Down

Not wanting to sound like a broken record, but wanting to be crystal clear on this point, he soldiered on...

Just knowing what is possible—knowing, seeing and realizing what others like you and I have done—breaks down any mental barriers about what we are capable of.

If this person can do this, I ought to at least be able to do that type of thinking explodes from this process.

I assure you this works, Counselor told us. His bill rate was proof, he smiled, half serious, half not.

Our challenge then is to determine what we want to do or improve upon and seek out those who have done it. There is no need to reinvent the wheel, just find who made the wheel and learn from them. Praccelerate! Accelerate your progress by expanding your perception of what is possible by seeking out those who have done it.

Another Way To Pracellerate

The first way to Pracellerate was to activate our *Pracell-Scanner.* We used this feature consciously to actively seek out Pracellerators, those who have accomplished or are accomplishing what we would like to accomplish; to recruit for our pit crew.

Sometimes, however, we don't know what we want to or can improve upon. It *may* be too tough to plan.

The second way to Pracellerate then, is to leave our Pracell-Scanner running. First activate it to seek out role models, but then leave it running to capture learning opportunities we just happen on by chance. Leave it running to detect those actions or behaviours that we either wish to emulate or want to make a note of to not emulate, that were not in the plan.

Leave it running, just in case.

The Pracell-Scanner therefore, has two features. One we activate to find Pracellerators, people we will be getting in touch with. The second feature is the constant scanning feature, the one we can activate now, that heightens our sensivity to behaviours, both positive and negative, that we stumble onto back accident, just by keeping our eyes peeled.

Like keeping an eye for change on the sidewalk, we actively watch for ways of thinking and acting that we might want to incorporate into our ways of thinking and acting.

We see people daily we can learn from. Random opportunities to learn abound. By watching and learning from other people's fortune, their setbacks, and their behaviour, we flatten out our learning curve. We take less time to get *there*.

Pracellerating is a choice. Role models live amongst us. They are us! We just need to be on the look out.

Easy To Criticize

Unfortunately, however, the feature switch of some of our Scanners over time devolves to *criticize and evaluate* from *congratulate and learn*. Like a tripped breaker in our fusebox, our *just lookin' at other folks viewer* sometimes just *flips* over to negative, detecting only what others do wrong, missing what others do right.

Our current scanners might send us the *is that ever goofy* part of what others do while it blocks out the *here is what can I learn from this person* part. It feeds us what's bad and blocks out what's good.

But it need not be that way. We can reset our Scanners, he said, having reset his and gained as a result. We can

---

become wide-eyed again. We can *sand off a few coats of life* to get back to that original state of *wonderment*, of being amazed and of learning quickly just by watching others. We can re-learn to lock in on the lessons and cut through the rest. The *reset* is a *choice*.

Because it is those people who are easiest to criticize who may have the most to offer; the ones we can learn the most from; the ones from whom we should most take note. We sometimes see only the *eccentric* when we could more benefit from locking in on what is *exceptional*.

An eighty year old cyclist rarely looks smooth, but they are the ones from whom the *most* can be learned.

So with a reset PracellScanner, rather than criticizing the *look*, we *learn* from the effort. Rather than detect what is goofy, we look for the good. Rather than look at what's wrong, we scan a little harder to find out what's right.

Unearthing the *good* takes a keener eye, more energy and the willingness to see what others won't. But it is a way of looking at things that energizes, uplifts and inspires, he observed and let sink in.

Good Luck or Good Planning

So whether it is by good luck or by good planning, whether we actively seek someone out or happen upon someone by chance, there is much to be learned. Learning from others is a wonderful skill and an informed choice.

And questions such as may I ask your advice and how did you do that become very powerful tools, ones that will honour those whose accomplishments we applaud and ones we can use to help us accelerate our progress, help us Pracellerate!

the brakes

W hile Pracellerating helps us make our own breaks, with some ways of looking at things we may need to apply the Brakes, he began.

Well said, we thought. We just didn't know what he was well-saying!

Pracellerating is a good thing, he continued. But with some ways of looking at things, we sometimes need to say *stop*.

And why, you may ask?

May?

Because we might be headed in the wrong direction, he answered for us.

We were all ears on this one.

The Brakes are what we use to help us stop using unproductive ways of looking at things. We stop, back up and continue on our way to *Easygoing*.

And there is one certain unproductive way of looking at things in particular that I would like to lock in on, he said somewhat extraterrestrially.

Beware the Force

And it was right then, just when we thought we had seen all the getups were going to see for a while, there he was, Obi-Wan Kenobi, cape, hood and all...

Beware the *force* he told us!

Beware the what, we asked?

The force, the Equity Force! He repeated, somehow expecting that we should know what he was talking about.

Beware the force of equity he began, because it can take us down the wrong road and severely sidetrack us on our journey to where we *Wannabe*.

This force *wills* us to look at others, make comparisons and then jump to negative and most times incorrect conclusions. And the result?

- our heart rate goes up
- we stew
- we feel hard done by
- we beat ourselves up
- we mistrust
- we presume the worst and lay blame
- we angst
- we talk *about* those we should be talking *to*

And we bring all of this upon ourselves by the choosing to go down this road, he told us. This *force* is a self-activating feature of our WorldProcessor, one that clicks on automatically unless we perform a manual override, he advised us.

Sounds formidable we said half-jokingly, but well more than half-not.

We can be our own worst enemy when it comes to wasting our emotion and wasting our time; of shining the light on the wrong spot when it comes to where we fix our attention. And a principle cause of this emotional drain is the *force*. Here is how it works:

On occasion, we look at others we feel we should be able to compare ourselves with. We look at their efforts and we look at their returns. This may or may not be what they are actually putting in or what they are actually getting out, but this is our perception of both. It is what we *think* they are giving and what we think they are getting.

We then compare *that* to *our* opinion of our own gives and gets, what we put into life and what we are getting in return.

We then make a *judgement* call. Are we being treated fairly, equitably, or is something out of whack? Does life seem to be fair or is it somehow not?

And on the strength, or weakness, as the case may be, of this very private, self-induced deliberation, we decide how we are going to feel, we decide how we are going to act. And the result of this force? We sometimes go off the road or even hit a wall. We are Brakeless in Intensity, a bad place to be.

This doesn't sound at all good, we repeated.

I assure you it is not, he continued, having been there before.

In the absence of the facts, we tend to jump to conclusions. We make presumptions and fill in the blanks. We fear the bad and assume the worst. We convince ourselves that we are being treated unfairly and our outlook follows the way. Our lens becomes clouded, we head the wrong way.

And this, he concluded, is the force at its energy-draining worst. We convince ourselves that others are being treated better, getting more while doing less.

And while not all of us are subject to this *force*, some of us unfortunately are, hence the need to *expose it*, to raise it to the level of consciousness, so we can put on the Brakes!

So the trick then? You are obviously way ahead of me, he confirmed as it was clear we knew where this was headed. We must learn to *use* the force and not let it *use us*.

When we look at others, we must see what we can learn, not cause ourselves to burn! We must put on the Brakes and turn ourselves around, stop the trip to Intensity and reorient toward Easygoing. Pracellerate, not degenerate.

He briefly continued, wanting to finish off this point...

A Pragmatic Assumption

It has been my experience, he said, that upon examination and analysis, after discovering other person's realities and their circumstances, after getting the facts of the case, that most times we stew and angst for nothing.

I typically discover that after going too far down the wrong road of assumptions, that what was or was not happening, what others were or were not getting, was fair and equitable. And that what did happen, should have happened, and that if it wasn't just right, it was going to be right.

And therefore, as a result of having made far too many incorrect negative assumptions in my day and having wasted far too much time, I personally have decided to rest on a fundamental belief that may or may not work for you but that helps me apply the Brakes.

And that belief is?

It is this. I choose to believe that, with very few exceptions, people try hard to do their best. I believe that what they earn, get, do, in the long run is what they properly deserve. And that if there are inequities, there must be good reasons and if there are inequities they will most likely be temporary.

This may be far too simple and for some even naïve, but I must confess, I adopt this perspective, I affix this lens, for very selfish and pragmatic reasons, he said.

This way of looking at things *wastes far less time*! Looking at the world this way expedites my journey. It helps me avoid mind-hogging detours and keeps me on the road.

I fundamentally believe that people don't *mean* to make mistakes. They happen, he said, we don't *mean* for things to go wrong. They just do. Inequities in life may occur. This has simply been my experience, he told us.

And quite honestly, he admitted, viewing the world any other way, simply eats up my time! Assuming the good, I spend no emotion. Accepting that there will be temporary inequities preserves my time.

However, and this was a big however...

When the *facts* tell me otherwise, spoken like a *gentleman*, I will protect my *honour*, he assured us. I will *then* invest the time and emotion necessary to see things made right. I will activate my Driver's Seat and then methodically move on.

And you kind of got the sense that as kind and gentle as Counselor was, you also got the sense that you wouldn't want to mess with him. Even at age seventy-five! He was straight-laced but streetwise, a little tongue-in-cheek but his eyes missed nothing.

My start-point, he reiterated, clicking back into *kind-Counselor* mode, is to assume the positive and proceed, rather than presume the negative and waste time. I focus on what I can control and let the rest be as it may.

So how do we learn to apply the Brakes?

Applying the Brakes

- we resist the temptation to make comparisons if we know it will take us down the wrong emotional road
- we presume the positive
- we picture ourselves making a conscious decision as to whether we will spend emotion on this issue, this person, or on this situation. With practice, it gets to be that simple
- we give others the benefit of the doubt to conserve our emotion - until the facts tell us otherwise
- we turn our attention to matters we control
- we are aware but not preoccupied, concerned but not worried
- in his best New York, Counselor suggested we *fawget about it*, that which we are stewing about
- we raise the existence of this force to our level of consciousness to be aware of if and/or how it affects us
- we consider a positive start point for what we assume about others—their motives, their accomplishments, how they got there
- we avoid jumping to conclusions
- we avoid drainers (those without Brakes, those who see the negative) and gravitate towards energizers (those who Pracellerate and can show us the way)
- we ask ourselves how productive this comparison really is

- we withhold judgement, see over, look past, get over, rise above

You're asking for a lot here Counselor, we told him.

I am well aware of that, he said. But knowing how to apply the Brakes better allows us to Pracellerate!

And remember, he reminded us, our *is* doesn't have to be our *could be* here, only better than our *was*. No one else's. Just ours.

the wedge

From the Brakes to the Wedge, let us now press on, he segued.

Better use of our Brakes helps makes things *safe*, he said; deploying the Wedge can help make things *better*.

The *Wedge* is another feature we can add to our WP. It is a feature I click onto several times a day, Counselor confessed. In fact, by adding the Wedge, we are able to upgrade our standard issue Clicker from Standard to Deeeluxe!

Step back! we yelled.

I'm serious, he enthused....

The Wedge is what we stick in between life's events and our reactions to them to give us time to decide what, if anything, we are going to do about them. It is the Stop button on the assembly line of life. It is how we interrupt our WorldProcessor long enough to make sure it is not producing *defects*. It allows us to slow things down so that we can better choose to decide how we will react to things.

Let me see if I can bring this concept to life, he said.

The Wedge is what we insert when:
- our kids decide to colour the walls with crayons
- we wish more time to ponder alternatives
- we get a flat
- the oil leak causes the engine light on the dash to illuminate, again!
- a button pops off when we are in a hurry
- milk spills
- we confront the challenges of every day life
- the *force* is with us, not in the good way
- we wish to reconfigure how we are looking at things

The Wedge simply gives us the time we need to deal with these in a more effective manner. Many times when we get stimulated, we just react! Once again, I should know, I have gone too quickly from situation to reaction more times than I care to recall, Counselor confessed. I may even have used *language*, but certainly not so loud that anyone would hear, he guffawed.

Oh, no Counselor, certainly not you!

Yes me, he cast his eyes down in remorse.

There have been times when I would get *stimulated* and go directly to *respond*. I would not stop at GO and would not collect two hundred dollars. It was straight action to reaction.

Where will this stop, we wondered out loud?

And then things changed, he calmed the crowd. My reaction time began to slow down and along with it, my heart rate. Not every time I got stimulated, and sometimes not as quickly as I would have liked, but my *is* got better than my *was*, as I continue to work to my *could be*.

I still visit *Intensity*, but on occasion now my kids even

call me Mr. Easygoing, he puffed out.

C'mon.

Serious.

The Question

So this begs the question, what is different between the times when I react poorly, and the times when my reaction is more controlled?

No Counselor, the *real* question is whether your kids actually call you that. He rarely allowed the facts to get in the way of a good story.

They do more so now than before, he trailed off smiling, as he continued.

It's an *equipment thing*, he went on. The difference in these instances is whether I remembered to insert the Wedge or not, he told us, equipment excuses coming by now as no surprise.

There can be a *wide expanse* between the things that happen and how we choose to react to them. *How* we respond to the life's events is largely up to us. And how we decide to behave is more of a choice than I had originally thought.

Certainly not rocket science, but years ago it was news to me, he confessed.

Over the years, I *learned* that most of the time, we can choose how we respond. I say most of the time because I still tend to react quickly, without much consideration or evaluation, when certain things happen. For example, when I miss the nail with the hammer, which is often, I still tend to just *react*.

Or when somebody gives me a *two-hander* playing

hockey, I still get a little snarly.

You *still* play, Counselor?

I'm the youngest guy in the league! he lied.

Over time however, I learned that *how* we react to things does not always have to be automatic. We can actively *process* what is happening, we can *step back*. We can interrupt the process, slow down our WorldProcessor, even stop the *line*.

We do so to better analyze what is going on, to look more objectively at what is happening, and *then* decide how we are going to proceed.

Pretty logical?

Sounds OK.

When the milk spills, we don't automatically have to explore the darker side of our vocabulary. It was an accident. We stick the Wedge in and decide how we'll react. We realize it's no big deal. We get a grip. We keep a grip. And life somehow goes on!

We have the capacity to stick the Wedge in between what is happening in our world and how we react to it. And that wedge is the *Wedge of choice*. This wedge serves as the separator, providing the distance and time we need to make better decisions.

We can *click* on to this feature any time we want. It is amazing how handy it becomes.

My experience and my observations show that in the absence of this Wedge, we automatically go from stimulation to reaction. Just visit any arena to see this borne out.

But once we know that we have a choice, how we react, becomes radically different. We are more measured, controlled and ultimately make better, more informed and more rational decisions.

It is as though we afford ourselves the luxury of an out of body experience, not that I have ever had one. And for the first time that day, he was *maybe* telling the truth.

We learn to *step back* or even *step outside* of ourselves to view the situation more objectively. The Wedge buys us the time we need to slow down and weigh the facts and make a rational decision when things don't go just right.

Cause If We're Breathin'

And why do we need the Wedge and the Clicker?

Because if we are living, if we are breathing, if we are trying to make a little headway, he said about as bluntly as he was about to say anything, sure as shootin' at one time or another, we're gonna make mistakes! Things are *gonna* go off the rails. So better to be ready for it and properly *equipped*, he exclaimed, as he pulled out his wooden Wedge.

From Standard to Deeeluxe

By stepping back and choosing how we'll feel or how we'll react, it's like taking our Clicker from standard issue and transforming it to the Deeeluxe Model.

With the Clicker, we control the volume of our voice inside, but adding the Wedge, we now start to control the voice's content and tone. We graduate to *this* type of internal dialogue:

Did something just happen that doesn't sit well. Yes?
Am I tempted to react in not a good way? Yes?
Should I? Probably not?
Or

Did I just do my best on something? Yes.

Was it perfect? No.

Did some things go off the rails? Yes.

Do I feel badly? Yes.

Did I mean for this or that to happen? No.

Will it end the world? Not likely.

Will I let this ruin my, my family's or anyone else's day, night, life?

I don't think so? Is it time to press on?

I think so.

The volume, tone and content of our voice inside begins to improve. And *we* are at the controls.

The Wedge In Action

The great ones in sports, it is said, are actually able to *slow things down*. This allows them to make better decisions, to let a pitch go by, or to anticipate what will happen next, he told us.

We had heard something about this.

Not that I would know, Counselor said.

Some things he *didn't* have to tell us.

Gretzky seems able to make time stand still. He seems able to fast forward things in his mind, replaying what is *about* to happen, if that's possible, and act on what he just learned. All while everybody else is operating in real time.

What seems like an instant to us is an eternity for him. He makes better decisions. He slows things down. He makes time stand still, Counselor said, unaware that one day even The Great One would retire.

We can slow things down too, he told us. We can literally and figuratively discipline ourselves to take the time we need to make better decisions; to react in a more controlled and informed manner; to plan our next moves. We can stop the *production process* long enough to ensure that the quality of our output—our reactions, our behaviour—is where we want it to be.

We can choose to decide to expand the space and time between when something happens to us and what we decide to do about it. We can add processing time and processing capacity!

An opportunity presents itself, we can now choose to decide how we'll feel about it and what we'll do about it. Or when we are presented with a challenge by deploying the Wedge, we afford ourselves the time we need to properly explore the consequences of the different ways we might address that challenge.

The Wedge, particularly when combined with the Clicker makes things safe; we get a grip, and then makes things better; we make informed choices about how to go forward.

When we get *stimulated* or upset or even when we're just a little *off*, the Wedge combined with our brand spankin' new, multi-featured Deeeluxe Clicker helps us:

- decide how we're gonna feel—it's a choice
- buy time
- slow things down to look at alternatives
- slow things down to explore the possibilities
- slow things down to allow us to *calm down*
- slow things down to allow us to be creative
- slow things down to look at the situation from others' points of view
- slow things down to allow us to make better decisions.

- call a time out
- *freeze* a situation long enough to figure out what to do about it
- make time stand still
- make better choices
- manage how we feel
- manage how we behave
- beat back the *force*

These are simply good tools for everyday living; good for repairs and handy for renovations.

Everyone agreed.

the gear shifter

W e had fun with this next Attitool, but I had no idea at the time how many different ways and how often I would end up using it.

He was back in race car driver outfit.

Ladies and gentlemen, start your engines.

Again?

Again.

In the race of life, during our daily routine, we need to use different gears to be successful. Sometimes forward, sometimes neutral, sometimes reverse, sometimes first, second, or third. You get the point.

Similarly there are three *gears*, three ways of communicating and relating, that come *standard* in our vehicles. They, once again, already exist and function in our WP. I just want to introduce you to them, raise them to the level of consciousness so we can

- know them when we see them, and
- know better how to use them

The different *gears* we either unconsciously or, now,

consciously can *shift* into relate to a theory of personality called Transactional Analysis, created by Eric Berne.

The underlying assumption of the work is that within all of us are three selves; our *parent*, our *adult* and our *child*. These persons, these three ways of communicating with ourselves and with others, are also known as *ego* states. You may have heard of this way of looking at things. Its origins date back to the late-forties, early-fifties.

The term Transactional Analysis implies that every time we communicate with others or with our selves within, it is a transaction that can be analyzed. We can analyze the transaction to see which *self* was deployed.

Our Selves

Again, we have three *selves*, three ways of communicating. The *first self* is the parent. The *parent* in us looks at the world much the same way we *perceived* our parents and other people senior and influential to us did. We can see how our *perceptual filter* kicks in and impacts on things.

The second *gear/mode/tape/self*, is the *adult*. The adult is the rational and objective self. It is the one that is very much *in control*. It looks at the facts and situations objectively. It is the mode we are usually in as we deal with the world, process the world and live our lives. This is the normal mode, the closest to *autopilot*, the one that gets us through the day; the one where our heart rate is normal.

It is also the one that ought to make decisions about which self to use or click onto. It doesn't always win out though. It is also the *self* we should deploy to determine what self others are using when they communicate with us.

This analytical self, the adult, is the one that provides us with the clearest, most accurate, most objective view of what is happening. No rose-coloured-glasses, biases managed. It has the clearest lens and displays the most accurate snapshot of the facts we can muster.

The adult self is very important because it is on the basis of information processed/filtered by our adult, that we decide which self to utilize; the parent, remain in the adult or shift into the third *gear*, the *child*.

Our *child* is what we were when we were young: how we felt, the many ways we behaved, how we reacted to things. And that child is still very much within us. It's the one who belly laughs, cries hard and gets hurt. It is our fun self.

We are all three persons, none better than the other, all capable of working together.

This Is Important

It is helpful to know that these three selves represent another personality dimension that drives how we perceive things; represents three ways that incoming information can be interpreted and three ways we can send messages.

And up until now, it is possible that these selves have evolved and been functioning in us, on their own, without our conscious attention. They have just been *there* up until now; running sometimes quietly, sometimes not, as another integral feature to our WP.

And because we may not have known they were there, we could not take full advantage of what they can do for us or to us. Knowing that they exist can add immense richness to our lives and also keep us out of some hot water.

Which Self?

Because we are now aware that there are three selves and that we can use our adult to choose which self to click onto, it is far easier to tell:
- which self we currently have running
- which self we ought to *click* on for any given situation
- which self the person or persons communicating with us have switched on when they communicate with us
- which self to *click* on to best deal with the persons we communicate with.

Each Self is Recognizable

Each self is recognizable, in ourselves and in others. Over time we will be able to almost instantly recognize when we and others are in our/their parent, our/their adult or our/their child. Remember, even when it is most difficult, the thinking is that we will get the best outcome by using our adult to decide which self to *deploy* to best manage the situation.

Dovetail

This way of looking at things dovetails nicely with the Wedge, and the Clicker. Clicking on to our adult is what allows us the *time* we talked about needing to make proper choices. Being in our adult allows us to spend more time proacting and planning and less time reacting and apologizing.

It is a feature that gives us choices as to how we process the world, how we perceive what is happening, what has happened, what could happen and what we decide to do. It is technology that allows us to decide how we will react and proact based on the clearer, more controlled perspective provided by this way of viewing things.

And again, these aren't really new ways. They are merely the same ways we communicated before except that they now have labels and *handles*. We can now recognize and get hold of them. We can go into or out of these modes more quickly because we now know they are there. We can *go to them* as opposed to *back into them*. We can chase them down, to use them as opposed to dealing with the aftermath of being in the wrong self at the wrong time, something we can't do if we don't know these selves exist.

Self Watching

So let us refine then, our capacity to recognize the selves. As with bird watching, we can *self watch*.

He was serious!

Bird watchers realize that each bird has defining and distinguishing characteristics to differentiate them. It is the same with the selves. So let's learn how to *self watch* he suggested...

You guessed it...

Eyes closed.

OK, open'em.

Counselor was now in his finest bird watching outfit; *hiker* shorts, ball cap turned backwards, and was lookin' through some really nice binoc's. He was using his *child* to teach us how to *site* parent behaviour, adult behaviour and child behaviour.

We also now realized that every time he changed his

get up, he was using *his child* to access *our child*. It let us have fun, but also got us on the same *channel*; to break down resistances, to help us learn!

Siting Checklist

Here is a checklist. We are probably in our parent mode:
- when we have our index finger pointing at someone, our head tilted down and our left eyebrow slightly raised
- when we *lay down the law*, when we *order around*
- when we *act* parental
- when we use phrases like *you know you ought to* or *you should know better*
- when we tell someone they are sitting too close to the TV and they *ought to be careful because it's not good for your eyes*, and *don't look at the sun during an eclipse or else!*
- when we tell our kids to *sit up straight* and *don't chew with your mouth open*, and so on and so on.

We are probably in our adult mode:
- when we are being logical
- when our voice is even and controlled
- when we rationally analyze the facts
- when we *discuss* and involve
- when we remain calm in the face of someone else being either in their parent or their child, which is an active choice on our part but not always easy to do
- when we decide against sitting too close to the TV because we *reason* that it wouldn't be good for our eyes

We are probably in our child mode:

- when we belly laugh or cry
- when we sit three inches from the TV cause we really, really want to see the show
- when we *obey*
- when we don't care what anybody thinks, because it doesn't really don on us to. It is when our Woptou Scanner is clicked to Off
- when we act like kids, unencumbered by societal expectations and group norms
- when we make that *noise* we can make by cupping our hands under our armpits and flapping really hard to see what kind of reaction we can get from the *adults*
- when we play a practical joke
- when the bottom lip comes out

As you can see, *none* of these behaviours or selves are age specific. We can do most all of these at any age. And clearly Counselor was a huge fan of spending as much time in his child as he could.

As Events Unfold

The parent, the adult and the child are not just ways of speaking but are *mindsets* that we adopt, ways of viewing things and doing things that we can choose to click onto or engage, depending on the situation. They are labels for our behaviour and filters through which we can view our world, gateways to self-discovery, also throughways to self-acceptance.

Applications of this Technology

He then walked us through the various ways he had seen this technology applied:

WITHIN US
To Understand What Drives Us

This technology allows us to *step back* to some extent to figure out why we do some of the things we do. We can use our adult to *scan*, analyze and evaluate the beliefs that we carry with us to see what effect they have on us and whether or not they are valid.

We can *scan* the beliefs and attitudes we carry with us about ourselves, about what we believe we are capable of, about others, and about how the world works, that have been central to our perspective, to ensure they are still productive.

We can step back long enough to see, to the extent that we can, *why* we are doing the things we are doing. We are not eliminating our beliefs and values. We are simply doing an audit; a validity, reality and productivity check. Do these beliefs energize or do they drain?

This audit process might include something along the lines of:

- Why do I do this? What beliefs, what tapes are playing that are causing me to think this way or act that way?
- What are the beliefs that up until now, I have accepted automatically that may be causing me to act or behave in one manner or another?
- What are the good parts of these beliefs, the parts I should hold with me because they energize and fortify me and which ones drain, are perhaps out of date, are even inaccurate, one's I should modify?

This *framework* for looking at how we function, operate, believe and act affords us the opportunity to use our adult to check the validity of what our child and parent feel and believe, and then upgrade the quality, tone and content of *these voices inside.*

Real Deeeluxe Clicker. Top of the line now, he assured us.

Self Control

Knowing this material helps with self-control. Inserting the Wedge is similar to consciously clicking on to the adult feature of our WP. This is a valuable self-control feature, especially when the person we are dealing with has either gone right into their child or right into their parent.

At times like this, our natural tendency is to *match their mode* and *go at it with them.* It is at this very juncture, however, that we are wise to simply go into our adult and remain rational until things calm down. Wait them out. Wait until they realize they have *gone somewhere where they shouldn't have* and *then* have a rational discussion.

Because you can X-ray their behaviour to see that they have clicked into child, it becomes easier to control *your* reaction.

To Have More Fun

The child is a wonderful place to spend time. Wherever and whenever possible, we might consider seeking opportunities to go there. It does wonders for the Pomtgr. But more on that in a minute.

AS A MOM OR DAD
To Be Aware of our Power and our Impact

Knowing that this way of looking at things existed helped me as a father, he explained. It gave me a far better appreciation for the impact I had and the tremendous responsibility that placed on my shoulders. I grew to have a better, more consciously aware sense for the role that *I* was to play in the development of the outlook, the WorldProcessor, that our kids would evolve.

Informed Reinforcing

And knowing this helped in all roles I assumed going forward, he said.

Because I now had a better sense for how closely what we say and do is watched as mother/father, leader, coach, teacher, volunteer, I could now better appreciate the influence we can have. We can help shape a positive self image, work to enhance self concept and help young people gain confidence by what we say and how we carry ourselves.

And unfortunately, by how we behave and by what we say, we can also have the opposite effect.

'Nuff said?

'Nuff said.

The power of a well placed *you did your best* and *we couldn't be more proud* should never be underestimated. It strengthens, it sustains, it reinforces.

It is an ingredient once incorporated that rarely leaves the recipe, fuel once added that rarely leaves the tank, a building block once installed that fortifies the foundation.

Mixing his analaphors, he was on a roll. And he could not have been more correct!

IN BUSINESS
Self Control

Self control again?

Again.

Using our adult to make choices about how we act and react to situations can be of immense value. Negotiating is a prime example.

To Negotiate More Effectively

It is a fairly common negotiating tactic and something people may do without even knowing they are doing it, but intimidation, for some, is a tactic they deploy in an attempt to get the upper hand. Sometimes it works. Sometimes it backfires. As always, it is a personal choice.

Counselor's intent was to give us the tools to X-ray, to see through, this tactic when it is used on us.

During negotiations, some folks may use their adult to *go to* their parent to *admonish the child. Or* they may choose to click onto their *child* to *appear* a little *out of control* while in fact they are remaining very much *in control.*

They may or may not be doing this knowingly. That largely depends on whether or not they know this way of looking at things exists, he smiled.

By being sensitive to these approaches, these tactics, we can simply, very calmly use our adult to observe the behaviour, consider our response, and remain in control of ourselves, the situation, and how, or if, we choose to respond.

The reality is that *it takes two to tango,* Counselor pointed out. And the best way to get people back in their adults, if we choose to do that, is to choose to remain in *our* adults.

It's actually kind of comical, he said, to watch folks rant and rave. Sometimes the calmer we remain, the more we choose to stay in our adult, the more they lose control of their ability to reason.

In negotiating, actively choosing which *self* to deploy and actively watching which *self* is being deployed *on us*, allows us to keep our cool and make better decisions.

To Create a Mood

You can also use this tool to knowingly create a mood.

Picture with me if you will the following, as I witnessed first hand, the event I re-tell here. My wife and I had driven to a theme resort with my daughter, her husband and their two children to spend a few days.

What occurred at lunch one day was most fascinating, as it revealed to me what I sensed was an application of this technology.

They were an interesting crew, this large crew that entered the restaurant. I even eavesdropped as they came in. I hope you will forgive me....

Table for seventeen please? one of them said.

Seventeen?

Yes, please.

It looked to me like there was one set of grandparents, four more couples, possibly their kids, and their husbands and wives, and then there were the grandchildren. At any rate, they all plopped down and looked exhausted, from their morning of touring.

Their server, who is key to this story, then came out to greet them and asked if they wished anything to drink before lunch. They ordered massive pops all around and then ordered their meals. I noticed the server, while taking their orders, was processing their responses at a far different level, however.

My guess is that, again, either knowingly or intuitively, he had the Self-Scanner feature of his WorldProcessor fully activated, humming in overdrive, scanning the situation, working extremely hard to get a read on the mood of that table, seeing who was who, who could take what, but mostly, which *self* each person in this party was in, or could be in with a little prodding. This servers' Self-Scanner was on full alert, full monitor, maximum sensitivity.

Having taken the order and completed his *scan*, he returned with the pops but he also returned *bearing arms*!

He was armed with straws, but not just any straws. He came back with the straws that were covered with paper sleeves. You know the ones. The ones that if you rip off the very tips and jam the paper a little, and apply oxygen vigorously to one end, you can turn the paper enveloped straw into a weapon, a paper projectile, harmless but effective.

As it turned out, this astute young server, in full view of us all, chose to do just that! He drew back his weapon, prepared to do battle and locked his sites not on one of the kids sitting there, but goodness forbid, on the Gramma!

I heard them all gasp Oh my gawd, not Gramma! Because they knew what she would do.

Silence enveloped the room. We hushed in anticipation as he continued.

But it was too late. This young man had made up his mind. He had his target.

Before *any* of us in the restaurant could stop him, because by now we were all involved, his ammo was released!

It released with an audible *hiss*.

The paper laser was en route, sailing three feet over the

table on a flat trajectory traveling approximately twenty miles per hour, but seeming much slower. It sliced through the warm summer air, cruising over plates, over pops, over heads. It cleared the salt and pepper shaker, over the centre piece and locked in on its target.

SSSSUUUUMMMMMMMMMAAAAACCCCKKKK!

Nailed her right on the forehead.

WELL!

The entire room fell even more silent. The entire *resort* fell silent! Waiters, customers, guests, the cook even peered through the glass opening to the kitchen.

What would Gramma do?

The server knew full well what she would do.

She glared at him.

She then, without missing a beat, prepared her weapon and returned fire, striking him with a direct hit. Felled him. And before we knew it, the entire room had erupted with paper crossfire and genuine belly laughs.

And all was right with the world.

And why did all of this happen?

I believe all this happened because this *kid*, this waiter knew how to get at *Gramma's kid*! Because our astute young observer read from the kibitzing at the table while he took their orders, that the biggest *kid* at the table was *Gramma* which is the highest compliment that Counselor felt a person could be paid; and through her, he could get to everyone's child.

People undertake all kinds of activities to access their child, whether we are aware of it or not. The *child* is a *great* place to be and all kinds of businesses could benefit from knowing how to get to it.

Just Knowing Helps

As with almost every one of these tools, he said once again, just *knowing* helps. And having this way, these ways, of looking at things now raised to the level of consciousness, we can make more active choices as to how we choose to behave.

Or in some cases, *not behave*, he said as he lowered himself onto the whoopee cushion someone had *just* placed on his chair.

the calculator

He began the discussion of his next Attitool a little sheepishly, a little uncomfortable with the topic but certain that it needed to be covered.

He took us right back to our *adult* with this one.

Your personal financial situation is absolutely none of my business, he correctly began, *very* much switching gears.

However, and this too was a *big* however, while your financial situation at first may seem like none of my business, we have agreed that your sense of well-being *is*, he recounted.

And because you and I both know that money affects our well-being, we would be remiss if we did not at least touch on the topic of money.

Are we agreed?

We are agreed, albeit a little reluctantly.

So with your permission, we will touch on it, then leave it as quickly as possible.

We had consensus.

Getting the Nest Egg

I am by no means an expert on this topic, he confessed. But if making mistakes along the way and learning from them in any way qualifies me to at least facilitate a discussion around dough, then hopefully I will be allowed that.

He was so allowed.

You will recall money being identified as one of the ingredients listed in the *famous one-hun*. Well let's get out our Calculator and deal with this head on.

I wish to discuss and share with you what I have seen work for others as it relates to managing their personal finances and building some form of retirement nest egg. Again, the reason we are discussing personal finance is because of its impact on our day-to-day well-being.

Money is the type of thing that doesn't affect us much if we are getting it right, but most definitely permeates our perspective and fogs up our lens if we are getting it wrong. I speak from experience, he said. Let us therefore spend some time on what we might do to get it right.

The Realities

Let's start with some realities of money, from my perspective that is, he cautioned:

There are Two Ways To Make Money

There are two ways to make money, he said. *Us* at work and *our money* at work. And the quicker and earlier we can get our money working for us, the more it will earn and the better for us.

The earlier we can start, the better. There is a concept called compounding. It means that our money can earn money on the money that it earns. That is the *money at work* part. So the earlier we can start the process of getting our money to earn money, the better.

Did I already mention that, he smiled wanting to drive home the point.

The good news, though, is that it is never too late to start, and we *can* make up for lost time. It is better to start early, although playing catch-up *can* be done.

He stepped aside for a moment. We all *know*, that we all *know* this stuff. *But*, as with medical checkups, we probably don't do a *financial checkup* as often as we should. Some of us might not do it at all!

But, as with our physical condition, we *need* to know. Because while we might seem fine for now, we need to look long term. And this is what this segment is all about.

We all looked at each other and him and agreed that while this might not be the most fun part of the day, we all knew that we needed to take our *medicine*, so we settled in.

Accumulating Money is About Making Choices

When I was younger, he said, I believed I did not have a choice about saving for retirement. I simply had too many expenses. It was out of my hands. Sound external? Am I sounding a bit like a passenger here?

I *couldn't* save for retirement, I had myself convinced. Well, as I reflect back on it, I did have enough on a month to month basis to at least *start* saving for retirement. I simply chose not to, although I didn't look at it that way, at the time.

Then, I chose power windows over saving for the long term. Not a bad thing and something many of us do. But the long term suffered at the expense of power windows and an overactive Woptou. I was buying things for show, instead of saving some of my dough, he confessed.

I recognize all too well that saving money is not as simple as I am making it out to sound, but at least philosophically, are we agreed that saving money is about making choices?

We agreed that it was.

We Are More Stabilized When We Are On A Plan

Another reality is that we feel increasingly out of control when we are not firmly in control, financially. And the more we are out of control, the *louder that voice inside* gets. We are *away* from *Easygoing* headed straight for *Intensity*. And this condition is not good for our longevity. We even begin to tie our self-worth to our net-worth. And the outcome is not positive.

Once we arrest the process, though, once we stop the line, turn the ship around, he Saidanotherwayed, all of the opposite reactions occur. The voice inside turns positive, the pressure eases. This particular life context ingredient no longer acts as a pebble in our shoe. Our sense of optimism returns. We no longer behave at work—cautious with what we say, tentative with how we act, reserved in what we recommend—in accordance with a negative bank balance. Been there, he commiserated. We work from a position of financial and emotional strength, acting on what's best as opposed to doing what's safest. Been *there* too, he reassured. The strength of our conviction rises with the number of month's salary we have set aside *just in case*. We are headed back to Easygoin. We're more confident, reassured, self-assured.

Money Buys Choices

Yet another reality is that money buys choices, nothing more, but certainly nothing less. It can also limit choices. It can be a painful source of frustration, distraction and pre-occupation. This one ingredient, *too much month left at the end of the money*, will *always* find a way to affect the overall taste of the recipe. It is a life context issue that affects much of what we do. And the reality is that no matter how hard we try to jam the Wedge of choice in to *decide how we feel* about too many bills, it can be an uphill battle.

So, What Do We Do?

So, what do we do, then?

Well, we can either change how we feel about our financial situation or we can change our financial situation. Or both. The liberty of the *And*, he reminded. We can change/improve the situation, get our financial house in order, *and* change how we view our situation. We can take charge!

For the next few minutes, Counselor gave us his thoughts based on observation and *having been there*.

To stimulate our thinking, he said, the following are some thoughts, observations and recommendations...

The Scanner Fade - An Observation

He had observed that the more in one's bank account the less active the Woptou Scanner. The scanner seems to lose power as people come closer to meeting their financial objectives. But not in a bad way. They seem to be kinder to people just because it is the right thing to do. As we touched on, their convictions strengthen because they worry less about the consequences of a *too accurate* recommendation. They lose less sleep over things that don't matter.

It's not that folks don't care when they are debt free, he said, it is that they feel more free to care about the things that *really* matter. They feel more free to speak their mind, to lend a hand.

Because they are less concerned about their own month-to-month, they are better able to ask about *other's* day-to-day.

More incentive to get it right...

Meeting Max

He then touched on some things to look out for, some things to plan for...

Because we are human and because we all have needs, there is a reasonable chance that we'll all meet Max, or at least come close to meeting him. We meet Max when the clerk says, I'm sorry but we can't process this transaction, you have *maxed* your credit limit.

Hello Max!

And how do we feel when we meet Max? Embarrassed. Ashamed. Our Woptou Scanner goes on overload. The dreaded Wdwtoo Scanner (*what do we think of ourselves*) even clicks in. And what it is telling us is not good. Our self worth *gaps* down. Yikes!

So how will we know when we are about to meet Max? How can we avoid having that meeting?

Anticipate! Know the stages in your life when he is

most likely to make an appearance. Do some planning. Make some choices.

There will be times in our lives when we almost *know* that the demand for dough will outstrip the supply, he observed.

Some of us wisecracked that that was just about every month. He smiled back knowing that was more true than any of us, including him, wanted to admit!

Our task then is to anticipate the expenses and avoid the potholes.

The needs are so predictable....

When We're At School
- tuition, books, rent, Kraft Dinner®
- maybe even a car

When We Get A Job
- clothes
- stereo, so we can relax when we get home from our new job
- some furniture
- Kraft Dinner® and weenies

As We Grow Older
- couple of rings and a honeymoon (Counselor warned the kids in the class that this may be the best vacation they will get until their twenty-fifth wedding anniversary, so he paternally encouraged them to enjoy it)
- more furniture
- insurance
- gas

- a house which equals a mortgage which equals a brand new state of mind all unto itself
- camcorder

If We Have Kids

- more furniture
- another car
- a van to cart the kids to lessons of every sort; figure skating, power skating, hockey, soccer, precision skating, dance, body checking school, dry land training, confirmation class, the show, the junior prom, band practice, basketball practice, volleyball practice, camp, and then to the college or university or job they choose to go to, at which point the nest empties
- money to repair our vehicles

When They Get Older

- money to help with the kids' education
- money to help the kids with all the stuff we just listed

When We Get Older

- vacations
- pay off the mortgage
- accelerate our retirement savings because we fell behind when the kids went to school
- new clubs and a plot, not necessarily in that order

These were expenses we could all relate to and expenses that are as predictable as the next day of the week. These occur, like clockwork, as we move through life, he said. So where possible, if possible, it is best to plan.

It was at that point that he flipped on his banker's light,

donned an accountant's visor and activated his Calculator.
It was time for action!

An Action Plan

So what do we do? Let us rearrange and reorient our
financial affairs so they become a source of peace and inspiration as opposed to a source of angst and consternation.

Counselor hated being consternated!

The key, he felt, to making that transition was crystal
clear in his mind. The key was to get to debt free.

Getting To Debt-Free

Going from meeting Max to debt-free, while being a
tough journey is a worthwhile one. It is an integral part of
the journey from *Intensity* to *Easygoing* as he once again,
pulled out his map.

Debt free is a terrific feeling, he said. We got there later
than we wanted, but what a feeling when we did, he said.
Freedom. Liberation. Pilot versus co-pilot. Driver, no
longer the passenger. Independent, not dependent!

Debt-free is darn near worry free, at least financially.
The second we get to *debt-free*, our Pomtgr jumps four levels. Water falls off our duck's back. Milk spills and no one
cries over it anymore. The Wedge pops in and we don't
even need it, he only slightly exaggerated.

We get just a little easier going. In fact, the moment we
create and begin implementing a plan to get debt-free our
Pomtgr jumps at least two levels. Been there, *too*,
Counselor assured us.

Increased peace of mind sets in as we get a handle on
the problem and as the treatments begin. We don't have to

be all the way cured to start benefiting or feeling the positive effects, he reassured us. Those start the minute we begin taking action.

Install the Calculator

So how do we improve our financial situation? How do we go from where we are now to where we would like to be financially?

There are nine action steps we can take to make progress.

Nine?

Nine quick ones, he fibbed.

For future reference we can also install these nine steps into our WorldProcessor. The *icon* that will come up on our screen will be a Calculator.

Step One—Hold Everything

Freeze the moment. Hold everything! We need to know our exact reality. We need to figure out our exact net worth (what we own versus what we owe), and our cash flow (how much comes in each month, exactly, less exactly how much goes out).

And when should we complete this exercise, Counselor?

Now is a very good time.

Now?

Right now! *Now* is always a good time to do anything.

Here is the format, he said. Use a piece of paper if you choose not to mark this up.

We settled in to fill in the blanks.

I had a pretty good idea where we were at, but it didn't

hurt to go through the exercise just to refresh my thinking...

Monthly Inflow/Outflow

Inflow

- Salary One
- Salary Two
- Other

   Total Monthly Inflow: _____

Outflow

- Mortgage
- Car Payment
- Car Payment
- Household Expenses
- Car Payment
- Credit Cards
- Loan Payments
- Food
- Entertainment
- Clothes
- Vacation
- Recreation
- Other
- Other
- Other

   Total Monthly Outflow: _____
   Leftovers (to Save/Invest/Pay Down Debt): _____

Net Worth

Assets:

1. Real Estate
2. RRSP's/401K's (U.S.)
3. Other Investments

    Total Assets: _____

Liabilities

• Mortgages
• Loans
• Credit Cards
• Other Amounts Owing

    Total Liabilities: _____
    Current Net Worth (Assets Minus Liabilities): _____

At this point you may be absolutely delighted, awfully disappointed or, like most of us, somewhere in between. The point is, however, you now know where you stand. We know *is*. Now let's get to *could be*.

Step Two—Run The Household Like a Business

The second step presents an option on how we can view our personal finances. It is a feature we can install into our WP. It can be a way of looking at our personal financial situation, a new filter through which to view the management of our money. It involves running our personal finances like we would run a business.

First make it safe, then make it better; we had heard that before, but it applied here as well:

- determine who in the household will be responsible for the administration of our financial affairs. One may have more of a *knack* for this kind of thing than the other. Assume responsibilities accordingly. Like in a business, assign responsibilities where strengths lie
- analyze spending patterns
- invest in infrastructure; filing cabinet, software, get organized
- buy a yellow highlighter and with it draw a line through each of those weekly mortgage payments to see how quickly progress is being made
- look at budget versus actuals on a month to month basis
- make personal saving a *corporate* norm, an objective, part of the culture, an expectation from all *staff members* at *the home office.*

As part of the Executive, you can call meetings on short notice and they can last only one minute if need be. The point is, though, that any good *business* communicates objectives and expectations, gets updates and monitors progress, actual to budget.

After you and your team have done all these wonderful things, though, you need to provide rewards. Perhaps milk and a cookie. Perhaps even two!

Control yourself, Counselor!

He smiled.

Step Three—Prepare An Action Plan

We need two action plans. One is the monthly plan, the short term outlook, the one we use to chart our month-to-month, and the one we use to calculate how quickly we can pay down debt. The other is a savings/retirement plan.

In one *we* are at *work*. With the savings plan, we put our *money* to *work*.

Balance the long term with being able to enjoy the present.

Step Four—Get Started

How we are doing financially is a chicken and egg/which comes first type of thing. The better positioned we are, the better positioned we are. They key though, as with most things, is to *get started*.

An object in motion stays in motion...

We had heard that before too, but *it* also applied.

Here were some suggestions on getting started:

- drive one of your existing vehicles *into the ground*. Vehicles are depreciating assets. They cost
- build equity; buy real estate, carefully of course
- pay down, or pay off, credit card balances
- if possible, start/build an RRSP/401K (U.S.)
- if possible, have your kids start their own RRSP *now* (or accumulate toward it if they are under 18) and have them put 10% (at a minimum) of whatever they earn into it. Almost without regard to the type of job they have or will have, if they follow this plan, by their mid to late forties, they will have accumulated a significant nest egg. Approximately $250,000, he said. Which in turn, with no further contribution, at an 8% return, grows to somewhere in the neighborhood of $500,000 by age 55, $735,000 by age 60 and well in excess of $1,000,000 by age 65.

That is what a savings plan, coupled with getting started early, and making a whole bunch of tough choices will do.

Counselor said he prepared a chart that showed his calculations and gave it to his kids to show to his grand kids. I am not trying to show my kids or grand kids how to get rich, he said. I am not the right person to do that. What *I am* trying to do is *show them how to accumulate enough money to be free to make choices.* I am trying to highlight one aspect of their lives they will need to manage to generate some peace of mind, or at a minimum, less grief. Money alone will not do it. But it also should not be ignored.

I hope my kids didn't mind and I hope they didn't think I was interfering, he winced, his Woptou mildly activated.

These action plans are designed to help us avoid the preoccupation and angst that grows out of not having a firm financial foundation and action plan. Again, *rich* isn't necessary, but we do need to know where we are at, be clear where we are headed and be satisfied that we are making headway.

It is more difficult to get *there* financially, if we don't have a plan. But just getting started on a plan, makes being *here* (where we are at now financially) easier, even if *here* is closer to *here* than it is to *there,* which is where we want *here* to be someday, he said, with that making perfect sense to him and not a lot to us.

Having a goal and a plan, and just getting started, will make us feel better, he summarized.

Step Five—Find Ways to Accelerate the Plan

- pay your mortgage off weekly as opposed to monthly
- destroy all but two credit cards
- pay them off each month
- develop a part-time hobby/business
- save more every month, even a little bit

Step Six—Aim For Two Targets

Aim for *debt free* as quickly as possible but balance that by contributing to a registered retirement savings plan as early and as often as possible.

This is a blatant repeat of Step Three, he said. We add it as Step Six because Step Three is so important.

We also add it because, having a long-term financial plan adds tremendously to our peace of mind. It adds even more as we act on that plan.

Step Seven—Accept the New Reality

Being able to *retire*, as our parents did, presumes we stay with one employer like our parents did, that we have pensions, like our parents may have had, and that the government will have payments for us, like they had for our parents.

Ladies and gentlemen, that paradigm, that perspective, may not be our reality. You most likely have had more than one employer, and if you do have a pension, it may not be enough. And as well, it may not be prudent to plan on any government assistance. We might rather view whatever comes from the government as a bonus.

The bottom line is that we might wish to presume that we will require some form of income generating capabilities well into our seventies, and if we end up having enough without it, then that too is a bonus. More vacations!

Presuming this even still though, is still a good idea. Remaining active keeps us energized.

Step Eight—Pass It On

"Managing Our Personal Finances" is a course and life

skill that most of us need to have, but few of us have had. And maybe it's not the easiest thing to talk about with the kids, but we do them no favours by not talking about it.

Pass *the basics* on to the kids, he suggested. Help them get started early. Starting them out with good financial habits and ways of looking at things will pay handsome dividends, he advised. It will allow them choices as they make their way down the road.

Step Nine - Better Late Than Never

Each and every one of our circumstances is different. *How* we are *where* we are is irrelevant. What happened before, we cannot change. How we go forward though, is very much in our hands.

Counselor Lived The New Reality

Counselor loved his work. We also suspect he was paid for what he did. He and his wife golfed in the summer, skied in the winter and both taught part-time at night.

It kept them young and involved, vital and making a difference. It also helped that it contributed to their monthly household bottom line.

Dividends

Our personal finances are just that Counselor reminded us, personal. They remain however under our control. So taking the time and effort to manage our *business*, to put us on a firm footing, to create a strong foundation pays immense dividends, financial as well as emotional.

He told us we could *bank* on it.

the venting licence

After all this talk about money and self-control and making choices, the pressure was starting to build. I think he was reading our minds...

When times get tough, he began, when *things happen*, when things well up, sometimes going Venting helps us get back on track. And that's OK, he suggested. But you can't go Venting without a licence, he sternly warned us.

He was now in full fishing gear. Hooks, lines, sinkers on his fishing vest, his favorite lure and some sea weed were dangling from his trusty old fishin' hat.

Sometimes life hands us things with which we must cope. And cope we will. But in the meantime, there is a very good chance that whatever happened caused us pain. There is also a reasonable chance that what happened may have caused us to anger, he understated.

And it was at times like this that Counselor was learning to go Venting. To go for just a few seconds to a quiet oasis in his mind, long enough to acknowledge that it hurt, and then very quickly press on. He told us this was an acquired skill. A skill to help us get by.

In fact, he even had a VL printed up. It read as follows:

Venting Licence

The holder of this licence is entitled to:
- ten steamboats
- nine shucks
- eight darnits
- seven long sighs
- six gees
- five triscrunches
- four Oh Wells
- three poor me's
- two why me's
- one very mild gosh darn it, or the term of the holder's choice, spoken completely silently to oneself, so no one can hear, when whatever happened to us really, really gets to us, so we can feel bad for a second without feeling bad, so we can harmlessly, yet properly, get whatever happened out of our system.

Restrictions
- we can't vent without licence
- we can't exceed our *limit* when we go venting, otherwise we get fined
- we can only vent at times and in places where it is impossible to do harm to ourselves, anyone or anything

This was a way of looking at things that allowed us to

feel the hurt of the child, but to manage our reaction to it in an adult sort of way.

Knowing we have a venting licence helps us:

- go somewhere else in our minds—go deep sea venting, even fly-venting; someplace peaceful and calm, for just a few seconds, while we get it together
- properly deal with the pain/anger/angst of a setback
- adjust/manage/relieve our cabin pressure in an orderly fashion while remaining in flight and remaining on course
- get over things
- manage the initial impact when things happen
- acknowledge that it happened
- successfully navigate the potholes
- buy time
- laugh at a situation that we ordinarily wouldn't
- put a smile back on our faces sooner than might ordinarily be the case
- carry on
- stay inside the lines, stay in control, while feeling, acknowledging and properly managing the pain
- catch ourselves, manage our emotions
- cushion the blow
- successfully diffuse a tense situation
- let the air out of the balloon slowly, as opposed to having it blow
- feel the pain of the kid in us, while keeping the composure of an adult
- pull in angsting time lines
- activate internal healing mechanisms
- *preserve* the *environment* while we let a little line out

The Venting Licence might be leaned on when:

- things happen
- we feel things getting out of hand
- we've been hurt
- we feel hard done by
- we need to relax
- we need to get over it

The Venting Licence, he told us, is a tongue in cheek way of recognizing that we are all human and that things sometimes get to us. It authorizes us to feel bad without feeling bad about feeling bad, provided we remain in control. It is the quick pause we need while we search for our Wedge.

The Venting Licence was also a not so subtle reminder that there are better ways to manage things when cabin pressure builds. It clearly sets limits and provides guidance on how to navigate through choppy waters without going overboard, he told us.

This Venting Licence, in fact may just be *the catch of the day*, he proudly announced, fumes from his fishing hat now rapidly filling the room.

Most noses pinched, we smiled and told him we'd already had our *fill*.

the jacket

Twelve down, nine to go. It was right after lunch, the aroma in the room thankfully back to normal...
Do you remember those cool reversible jackets you could get in the early sixties, he asked? Our kids wore them.

Some of us went blank. The sixties? Others went, Of course we remember!

He had one on.

You know the kind, he continued. The kind that are one colour on the inside and one colour on the outside and if you turn it inside out, it's like having two jackets?

Sure we said, looking at our fellow class mates, rolling our eyes *way* back this time.

The next tool I would like to introduce you to is the Jacket, a.k.a. the Reverser. It is a tool we can use to help us understand ourselves and others, and help us read what others really want.

We were a little delirious, and frankly a little groggy by now, but we were trying to hang in. We had eaten late and were fighting to stay with him. He, of course, had jogged, then had a muffin and some juice.

The Jacket stems from the premise that sometimes, often times, questions are not questions at all, rather they are statements.

The hook was in. He had us back. We were paying attention. But what was he talking about?

Are *you* cold? No, but *you* might be, if you are asking me that question, he said, again somewhere from nowhere.

Do you *really* like that colour? I'm not sure, but because you are asking me that question, in that way, there is a reasonably good chance that you have concerns about it, so we'd better discuss it, is the way the ensuing self-talk would go, he laboured.

We don't mean to be that transparent or easy to read, but sometimes we just *are*. Because sometimes, *the questions we ask* or the questions that others ask of us, are not questions at all, rather they are *statements*, he made clear; really us telling others what we *really* think by virtue of the questions we ask.

It is not *always* the case, but it happens enough times that sensitivity to it on our part, when others ask us questions, might really help us better understand what they want or need from us.

Questions are clearly not always statements. Questions are questions most times. *But*, he said, when we think they might be statements, we ought to click on the Jacket, and turn the question inside out, reverse it, to help interpret the message.

Deploying this feature of our WorldProcessor just might help us better relate to what other people are really trying to tell us. Looking at questions this way may trigger dialogue.

Having this type of *interpersonal radar* simply helps. This *query flipper*/question analyzer helps us be more sensitive to others we interact with: our families, our customers, our clients, our prospects and our co-workers.

The Jacket *may* help us *cut through* and *see through*, to what really matters. Counselor found this to be a valuable tool and kept it in his *everyday toolkit*.

You can see the applications in many walks of life, he continued.

When a prospect asks a salesperson how much the item costs, he may really be *stating* that money is a factor and he's thinking he might buy. When the prospect asks about delivery date, it may be time to get out the sun screen because a big order and a trip to the south can't be too far away.

Whenever an interviewer listens to candidate questions, he may pick up valuable nuggets of gold about the candidate's intentions, concerns and attitude. A question such as *Is it acceptable with security if I work literally around the clock every night*? if asked with some degree of sincerity, can be somewhat revealing, he smiled, making his point.

We all use this *reversal* process intuitively anyway. By turning what we do unconsciously—reverse the question—into something we can actively deploy at *will*, we may increase our effectiveness at understanding and relating to ourselves and others.

When we ask questions, Counselor pondered, are we really making statements? Questions like *do you really think that is a good idea* or *are you really going to wear that tie*, especially if accompanied by the type of body language that we could imagine, and most especially if *really* is pronounced with four syllables, are not questions, *they* are statements.

Kids Know

Kids know better than anyone, he said, that questions, especially from their parents, aren't really questions at all. Kids, he said, wrote the book on reversing a question. They can see through questions for what they *really* are.

When their parents ask:
What time will you be home?
Are you really thinking of that?

Kids know parents are really saying:
Don't be late.
Don't do that.

Or maybe kids just *think* they know. Because even if they think we are saying *don't be late* or *don't do that*, what we both know we are really saying is that we love you more than anything and we simply want you to be careful.

On second thought, maybe they do know! Counselor mused, lost in thought just for a second.

Re-engaged, he pressed on...

When our boss happens by and asks how the report is coming along, we might want to click on the Jacket. Maybe we should throw our Jacket on when we are trying to better read our customers. Those relationships can sometimes get a little *chilly* and we can use all the help we can get.

There's gold in them thar hills, provided we know which way to point our antennae, he encouraged in classic analaphor. Hidden within the hills of questions people pose may be the type of feedback, input, concerns, feelings and suggestions we really need, but that those same questioners may be reluctant to provide.

The more polite the person, the more we need to activate the Jacket, the more we need to be sensitive to their questions, he suggested.

Some people tell us how they feel, other people *ask* us how they feel.

He poured *that* to the top of our glasses and then let it drift to the bottom. Like chocolate powder first sprinkled on the top of a cold glass of milk, it sat there for a while, then it sunk in.

The Jacket can help us see things more clearly, he concluded. We intuitively deploy it anyway. We have always known that *are you sure you really want to do that* is the farthest thing there is from a question. So why not simply raise this process to the level of consciousness, as we are doing with most every Attitool, and use it to our benefit and to the benefit of those around us.

Don't you think that would be a good idea? Counselor asked.

It was clear, as we *reversed* his question, that *he* did!

the extension cord

The lights go off. The odd shriek...

Anybody blow a fuse in here? his flashlight a flickering.

He flips the lights back on. We rub our eyes. He's an electrician now. Amp meter, fuse box, you know, the works.

What is it, ladies and gentlemen, that can extend something while at the same time, charge it up?

None of us was sure, the question, as usual, coming right out of left field.

Anybody?

Nope.

The right answer would be an extension cord. An extension cord extends the reach of a cord and it also powers stuff up.

We moaned a little on this one, but listened anyway...

So why do we need an extension cord? Because we need to figure out what *extends* the length of *our* stay here and what keeps *us* charged up, he answered his own question.

What we are talking about here, is how to *live* longer,

he finally told us.

Oh, so that's what you're driving at?

Absolutely, he enthused, *still* goin'.

What are the keys to living longer? Is there a filter through which we can view the world, an Attitool that we can embed in our WP to help us do that? I think there is!

Counselor had a funny way of getting to the root of things. Live longer? How do we do it? It made sense to consider.

Well I'm not so sure it's as easy as that, he continued. Fact is, I can guarantee it's not based on what I've seen, but there may be some common *cords* running through those who have been able to do it; by those who have had an *extended stay* here at the *Hotel of Life*; a common thread that seems not to run through those who experience *early check out*.

And we may consider adapting these ways of thinking into our WP as a start-point for being granted an extended stay; to experience *late check out*.

He reported having done *extensive* research into the topic. However, the twinkle in his eye coupled with that occasionally present mischievous smile, left little doubt that he encouraged a wide definition of extensive. It didn't matter though. He was seventy-five; he had earned his stripes. More importantly though, by now he had earned our trust.

Fact is, his main intent was to get us thinking about longevity.

Kidding aside, he went on to present his observations as to the common threads among people who have been able to *stay alive* based on what he had observed. And he had a bird's eye view on this one. His PracellScanner, the one he used to scan for random learning opportunities, had been activated for years.

They Want To Stay Alive

Those who enjoy an extended stay here *want* to stick around. This is almost too simple, he said, but some people would rather not be on this planet and, as a result, behave accordingly. This choice is either conscious or unconscious. They may just not like how things are going at the time. The upshot is that they end up doing things to their minds and bodies that are counterproductive to longevity. They do way too much of what they ought not do, and way too little of what they ought to.

The flip side of course is that those who want to stay around tend to make the choices that naturally and inevitably align with that mindset.

They Are Passionate People

People who stick around here tend to be passionate. Passionate about something. Passionate about anything! It doesn't seem to matter what that anything is: learning, woodworking, reading, their businesses, their kids, grandkids, bridge, weightlifting, a favourite talk show. The point is, they are passionate about something.

There is something to look forward to as opposed to just something to look back on. They hook themselves to something that pulls them forward, something that yanks them out of bed each day.

They Stay With The Times

They have stayed *engaged*. They are still *checked* in to the hotel of life. They are still current.

They know the Beatles broke up.

They did? Counselor joked.

They Do The Right Thing

They have developed clear operating guidelines in their lives as to what the right thing to do is. Their sense of right and wrong and what ought to, and what ought not to be done, has fully evolved. They don't *waste* emotion.

Their Woptou Scanner Becomes Focused

Their Woptou Scanner remains activated but trained only on those who matter. Those who have been around for a while, tend to have sorted out what's important and what isn't.

They Take Care of Themselves

The folks that I have observed were not saints, he said. On the other hand, they did appear to have a reasonably healthy relationship with their body.

They feed it well and exercise it from time to time.

Chicken and Egg

All of the common cords that I just mentioned seem to result both in and from increased energy levels and positive lifestyle habits. It seems to be a chicken and egg thing. Having a purpose and a passion coupled with wanting to stick around seems to do the trick.

I ought to know, he said, I am as you know, seventy-four years young.

Counselor!, we reprimanded.

OK, seventy-five.

Can we see your birth certificate?

I think *not*! he smiled, let's take a stretch...

the shingle

One of the best ways I know to *build* your business, Counselor began, is to hang your Shingle; to adopt the perspective that you are in your *own* business.

But we're *not* in our own business, someone piped up.

You are absolutely right, he conceded momentarily, but you can be, *if* you so choose, he offered right back.

We unscrew the old lens and latch on the new.

Self-optmometrize?

Exactly!

The Shingle I give you now to download into your WP's, to affix as a new lens, is designed to serve as a reminder of a different way of viewing things, a different way of viewing ourselves and our jobs. It places you in the Driver's Seat and helps give you back control.

Lemonade 5 Cents

From the time we were kids, many of us saw ourselves as being in our own business, he stated, turning over his Lemonade 5 Cents sign. And from observing those who have accomplished much in their time here, he noted that they *took charge* of their own destiny.

Whether they worked for large corporations, volunteer organizations or had their own businesses; whatever their vocation, whatever their level, they ran whatever they ran with passion and they ran it as their *own*. They took risks.

Presuming we are *running* our own show infuses a sense of urgency he felt. It makes our decision making clearer. Will what I am doing right this instant better serve my customers and help build my business, or will it not? Yes or no?

We cut through. Decisions become clear.

From the dawn of time, we have had to be self-reliant, hunter, gatherers. Only recently in the grand scheme of things, has the *work in the office, report to someone else* perspective become more common. In days gone by, it was always an exchange; something someone *had* in exchange for something someone else *wanted*, a buyer and a seller.

And nothing, to my mind, has changed, he said. We *all* still have customers and we are *all* still service providers. So we are all, therefore, in our own business!

We were starting to buy in, the logic was tough to argue...

A Shift in Perspective

Adopting this way of doing and viewing things can change:

How We Think

• we reorient ourselves away from *working for someone* toward providing a product or service to our customers,

giving us a higher sense of purpose
- our boss becomes our most important *client* - it's easier to serve a client than report to a boss
- the people reporting to us become *our* most important *customers* because it is through them that we get our results
- our paycheque, benefits and bonus become our *revenue* stream
- we become more patient and also more passionate, we *own* this business; it is no longer *the* company, it becomes *my* company
- we look to over-serve
- our work station becomes our place of business, our base of operations, our World Headquarters, the nerve-centre for what we are to accomplish
- we feel far more in control of our destiny because we choose our business and we choose our customers
- we go from passenger to driver because *we* run the show
- we feel an increased sense of autonomy *and* responsibility
- we concentrate on serving the customer, not ourselves
- we are part of the solution because being part of the problem isn't good for business
- we look at what's possible: what builds the business as opposed to what's not possible and what brings it down

How We Act

- we sit at the front of the class because we don't want to miss a thing
- we invest more wisely: our time, our attention, our emotion, our money
- we speak our minds

- we serve others, and in so doing, better serve ourselves
- we influence as opposed to order, ask as opposed to demand. That way we get *repeat business.*
- we prioritize more effectively. It becomes easier to figure out what is important and what is petty, what serves our customer and what simply wastes our time
- we come in earlier and stay later
- we choose our *associates* wisely

What We Get

- people gravitate toward us because *we* make things happen
- an immense amount of pride and satisfaction from a job way more than well done
- more business, perhaps more rewards
- word of mouth referrals
- an increased sense of well-being and personal dignity

Debugger

As with other Attitools, the Shingle can serve as an upgrade for our WP. The Shingle makes us revisit things, take a second look at our operation. Are there any assumptions or perspectives currently running in our existing WP, that we might wish to delete, upgrade or replace? Are there existing ways we are looking at things; our jobs, our co-workers, the boss, the people we serve, that could use an upgrade?

Building Our Business

So how do we *build* our business? We can build our business by:

What We Know

- our knowledge about our chosen area of expertise builds business. Are we continually upgrading, taking courses, reading, renewing, refreshing, looking for different ways to add value by serving as a resource, whether we are twenty-one or seventy-one?
- knowing our strengths and weaknesses, what makes us different, unique, in demand, our *competitive advantage*
- knowing that word-of-mouth is the most effective way to build a business and that good service builds a positive reputation that creates positive word-of-mouth referrals/recommendations
- knowing that news of good service travels fast, and high, but that news of bad service sometimes travels *faster* and just as high
- knowing that first impressions are critical and we only have one chance to create one (the first day on the job, the customer really wants to be served well because they made the decision to retain our services)
- recognizing who our *real* customers are and what they want

What We Do

We can also build our business by:

- giving the customer what he or she wants, not just what we have; It is the difference between what would you *like* versus here is what I *have*!
- taking every step possible to ensure repeat business
- positioning ourselves as a resource (which grows out of our knowledge; our knowledge about the company, product, market share, technology, competitors, sales

levels, everything, even if we are junior and even if we are new—all of which you control)

He was pretty adamant about this knowledge thing...

- looking for opportunities to add value
- when a *client* calls asking for more, sooner, accepting the call enthusiastically and then delivering far more than was asked for far sooner than expected
- creating personal service standards for our service, creating them ourself and ensuring that they *exceed* client expectations.
- installing quality controls and soliciting *customer* feedback.
- setting goals
- being effective (doing the *right things*) and efficient (doing them the *right way*)
- asking what would I do if this were my own business whenever we have to make a judgment call
- choosing our customers wisely

Sweating the Details

- by assuming an internal perspective. *We* determine the quality of our service, the type of approach we use, the attitude we bring, even in the face of *tough customers.*
- by appreciating that *every time* a customer comes into contact with us, our service, our products, they are drawing conclusions and making decisions about whether to reorder, refer, come back, rehire, retain, promote. It sounds harsh. It is also the truth!
- by answering the phone the way we would like to hear someone answer the phone and in a way that leaves no doubt we want to build our business (no matter what just

happened before the phone rang)

- by dressing accordingly; Of course accordingly could mean jeans in this day and age, Counselor acknowledged, remaining with the times
- by making sure World Headquarters, our work area, is appealing to our client base
- by making sure the nature, tone and quality of our communication, written and verbal, reflects the quality image we want to create for our business
- by treating customers politely and with respect, even if they occasionally do not return the courtesy

Counselor left no doubt in anyone's mind that building one's business is a choice. It is up to us. What we know, what we learn, what we do and how we do it are all choices. How much we sweat and how much energy we spend is completely in our hands and no one else's, he insisted. And without regard to our revenue source, a weekly salary or as a result of a product sale, the same principles for business building most *definitely* apply.

Sizzle and Steak

It is not only what you do but how you do it, Counselor continued. I know you know this and we may not like it but it needs to be said, he said.

Sizzle however, without steak, and smoke without fire, and style without substance don't pass muster. None of the former are effective without equal amounts of the latter, he reinforced. In the short run, perhaps. In the long run, never! When we serve our customers, both *what we do* and *how we do it*, has importance in our customers' eyes. As we all know;

- if the food was great but the service terrible, we will choose not to go back
- if the report is on time but of poor quality, we are only getting it partially right
- if the product is of high quality, but the service delivery negative, *that's* not good for business
- if the essay is terrific, but one day late, *that's* not good for business
- if the *output* was great but the *outlook* substandard, we will look to others to help us get it done the next time around

We must fire on all cylinders to get it just right. *What* we do, *when* we do it and *how* we do it are all factored in by our clients, either consciously or unconsciously. Those are the rules of business, survival of the fittest. Counselor was now Adam Smith, the father of Capitalism!

If performance exceeds expectations, we will almost always succeed, he succinctly concluded.

Hard To Listen Too

Counselor confessed that much of what he had just talked about may have been hard to listen to.

I know that what I just said may have sounded a bit extreme, and to some, maybe even unreasonable.

But this ain't charm school, this is reality, he chortled half-joking but more serious than not. What I am simply suggesting is an upbeat way of looking at things that can add zest and vitality to how we approach our working lives. It is also a way of differentiating your *product* and maybe even getting your name on the top fifty fastest growing list!

Hanging Your Shingle

Presuming that we are running our own show, presuming that we all have customers, and presuming that there are no guarantees can take us and our businesses to new levels, he submitted.

So hang your Shingle, he suggested just one more time.

You never know, he said, it just might be good for business!

the seat belt

S eat belt Grampa!
Seat belt?

Yeah, Grampa, you don't have your seat belt on, my young Grandson pointed out several years ago, in a how-could-you-not and I'd-really-like-it-if-you-would kind of way.

And ever since then, when I get in my car, I try to remember to buckle up.

But that got me thinking.

Everything gets you thinking, Counselor. About what though?

About habits. About how they are formed and how they are broken; which led to the development of Attitool Sixteen, the Seat Belt.

How could a two-word statement from a child get a sometimes stubborn seventy-five year old man to change a habit? he pondered.

Sometimes stubborn? we kidded him...

Let me digress, he digressed, ignoring our question.

It may be easier to find a cure for the common cold than it is for an adult to change a habit.

Just think about it for a second. How many sugars we have in our coffee, the route we take to work; our daily routines, are very much ingrained. For us to change any of these would not be easy. But just because it isn't easy, doesn't mean we shouldn't try, correct? he said.

Correct.

And while we're at it, let's also expand our definition of a habit. I used to look at habits as simply physical acts. But the more I thought about it, the more I realized *how* we consistently, almost automatically look at things, can also be habits. So let's consider both our behavioural as well as our attitudinal habits as we look at the process of making and breaking habits.

Digression, digressed, let me now get back to my original example. Believe it or not, he began, there was a time when seat belts were not worn. Why, when I was young, he served, they were not even invented, so it was never really on my radar to buckle up.

They had cars when you were young? we volleyed.

Without a doubt, he returned for the winner, all of us smiling.

So it was my grandson who triggered my behaviour change - helped me start the habit of wearing a seat belt! It was he who first observed that I didn't wear one. And it has been ever since the first Seat belt, Grampa, that I have been trying to improve. And while my *is* isn't my *could be*, he said.

It is better than your *was*, we finished again for him.

I believe you *have it*, he reinforced, clearly pleased.

Changing Habits

As I mentioned, I sensed that this behaviour change could teach me some things about habit change. I, therefore, *distilled* up what I learned about *the process of changing that habit* and offer the steps to you here:

Step One—Awareness

I became aware that there was a habit that needed changing. I didn't know it before.

And this step was the most important. I was oblivious to the behaviour and oblivious to its impact. It simply wasn't on my radar.

So, Step One is critical. It helps us identify what to change. Steps Two through Six help us with how to change.

He now had a mechanic's outfit on, complete with coveralls and rags.

Creating awareness around the habits we need to change requires meticulous self-discovery. And to do that, I have a special device. It is called the Habitomometer.

The what?

The Habitomometer, he replied.

That's lame, we teased him.

'Twas the best I could come up with. Gimme a break. We were all smiling now.

Just pull your habits, the ways you routinely do things and look at things, over here so I can hook you up.

Me? Yes You! Ah, geez. Here we go again...

It was easier to be singled out this time though, even though it hurt a little when he fastened it to my forehead.

Now lets run your habits through this thing. If the reading is green, the habit we are measuring is one that energizes and helps as we head to *Easygoing*; it's a keeper, no adjustments necessary. If, on the other hand, the Habitomometer flashes red, then we're gonna have to do maintenance on the habit, upgrade our approach or replace it altogether, he said, rag out, wiping his hands.

By now we were numb.

Step Two—Importance

Once we identify the drainers, we then need to look at making a change. We will only make the change though if we view the change as being worthwhile; the *get* justifying the *give* or the *give up*. The more importance we assign to it, the easier it is to change. So look at the effect. How is what I am doing or how I am looking at things affecting the *engine*, ours and those around us? How significant is the impact?

Is it getting us to *Easygoing* or is the behaviour causing us to stall?

Click on the Wiifm Scanner. How much is in it for us to change? What is the cost if we don't? If the cost is high enough and the benefit strong enough, if the meter is red enough, then the change is a must.

We can also click on our Whto Scanner, our *what happens to others* Scanner to help with the change. It highlights for us the impact of what we are doing and how we are looking at things on those around us.

So, all of these Scanners can tell us the habits that work and the habits that don't. The price that is being paid as well as the price that needs or could be paid if we stay where we are at.

Step Three—Make the Change

Once we find out what we need to change and understand its importance, we then make the change. We adopt the new behaviour, we try the new way. We adopt the new system, try the new grip. We get proper instruction though, to give it a chance.

Step Four—Repeat, Remind and Give It Time

For a behaviour to change the behaviour must be repeated, or repeatedly not repeated as the case may be, he so eloquently stated. Step Four, then, is three steps in one. Repeat, remind and resolve that you'll stay with it. To do this we need to tap our voice inside on the shoulder. Give the new way of operating a little R, R and R. Repeat, remind, resolve! Repeat the new behaviour and remind ourselves why we're doing this. And *then* stay with it, at least for a month. Because as we make the transition, we may even take a few steps back. One step back, two steps forward.

Step Five—Reward

With Step Five, we reward. Repeat, remind, resolve, then reward. Find a reward for the behaviour change. The reward could be that we just feel good. Or simply live longer. The reward could be a job better done or the kids looking up to us. New doors being opened or a bowl of ice cream.

Give yourself a pat on the back, he smiled, foretelling his last Attitool, it is always well worth it. The rewards might be all of these, but make sure they are at least some of these.

Step Six—Accept

We may not be perfect yet but we have made a start!

I mentioned at first that I buckle up most times. Sometimes I forget. Sometimes I revert. My behaviour change is not one hundred percent yet. But my *is*, is better than my *was*. Remembering my seatbelt most times is far better than not at all.

Step Seven—Improve

Once we see what is possible, we see what is *possible*. Now that I'm at eighty percent with my seat belt, ninety percent comes more easily into view.

Once we establish a habit, it is amazing how we are able to improve.

Pulling his rag out and wiping his hands, he tried to finish off.

This habit business is always tough work, but now that we've dealt with it, I think you'll be pleased with your improved *performance*.

He then began preparing to introduce the next tool but I had to interrupt.

'Scuse me.

Yes?

Are you going to unhook this thing or what?

Sorry, about that, he said, but as he did, he sort of whispered just loud enough so that everyone could hear...

There was a severe red signal that came up when I hooked you up but I didn't want to say anything. Something about this habit you have of missing four footers on the back nine, he joked.

Unfortunately he didn't know that *that* was no *joke*!

the incubator

His next get-up was a green skull cap and mask. He had a stethoscope in one hand and cruise brochure in the other. Western Mediterranean.

His diagnosis? In some cases, he said, we are best to use the Incubator.

Is it serious, Doctor? we asked.

Very, he confirmed, in his most *medical* tone.

You know the brain is a funny thing, he began. It is the size of a grapefruit and weighs only a couple of pounds. What's interesting, though, is that we reportedly use only ten percent of the brain's capacity. And with all this extra horsepower, underutilized RAM or ROM or whatever that is, it seems to me we have an opportunity.

There is a process called incubation that we can deploy to use some of that extra capacity; make far better use of our time, and allow us to multi-task without much additional effort. The brain automatically incubates for us. Our task is to simply recognize that the brain is capable of this process and to trigger it at will.

We have this extra capacity/processing power just sitting there and all we have to do to utilize it is to know it exists and then *feed* it; give it something to chew on and let it work its magic.

This incubation is obviously of the *thinking* kind as *opposed to* the *baby* kind although there are similarities.

Incubating, up until now, may have been an automatic, unconscious process. It is another feature of our WorldProcessor that we now raise to the level of consciousness for our use; to use proactively, to deploy when appropriate. Before, we would see only the output of what the brain automatically does for us. We were incubating and we were enjoying the results of it, but as with many of these processes, we didn't know why or how it was happening. We were competent, but unconscious as to why.

We would just, after sleeping on an issue, *get* these *results*. And there is a very good chance we wouldn't know how to make *that* happen again. We would get to a neat place, but not know how to get back there again. Now we do! Now we can! From here on in, we can be aware that we have this capacity to incubate and the capacity to deploy it at will.

Counselor bristled at underutilized processing power and excess capacity.

Chile Con Carne

It was then that Counselor opened the side doors to our seminar room and the catering staff paraded in, on cue, just like the closing dinner on a cruise ship, and placed in front of each of us two small cups of chile con carne. Nothing was flaming thank goodness.

One was a red cup, the other one was blue.

Please taste each of these, he asked, and mark down which one you prefer.

We all just smiled and went along with him at this point. We couldn't recall ever being served quite like this. He had attended to the details. Excellent customer service!

Counselor had his own special way of burning things into our memories. Like the string tied around our finger to help us remember something when we were kids, he would stop at nothing to get us to remember a concept or idea. To get us to remember the process of incubation, he brought in the chile.

Which was your favorite? he asked.

The red cup was voted unanimously superior to the blue.

Just as I suspected, he said, as he held up a sheet of paper where he had already marked down his expected tally.

To make a great chile, you begin with green peppers, onions, hamburger and if you wish to start a global debate, perhaps even beans.

You then throw all of these ingredients into a pot and *let it simmer*. That's the key. You let it *come together*, distill, meld, marry, combine, synergize. The things that happen in that chile pot as you know, he said, can be magical, even mystical.

The Point

His point was this, though. If you were to serve the chile immediately after preparation, it would be good.

However, he said, if you let it *sit* in the refrigerator

overnight and have it the next day, with nice warm buns and butter and a huge glass of milk; in other words if you let it incubate further, overnight, the quality, the taste is far better than it was the day before.

The red cup of chile, as you have probably already surmised, was prepared last evening; whereas the blue cup had been prepared only minutes ago. Hence the impact of incubation, the power of simmering.

To Activate Your Incubator

The incubation process can be proactively, consciously activated to allow our subconscious, our processing power, to work its magic. Incubation helps us find answers to things we didn't think had answers. Incubation helps us solve problems and produce creative solutions.

It is as simple as *this*, to activate the incubator:

Step One—Figure Out What to Cook

Identify the issue you want to *cook/simmer/incubate*. Identify what you would like to give some thought to.

Step Two—Load In The Ingredients

Load up your mind with all relevant background material. Read the report. Read the research. Add the ingredients.

Step Three—Stir

Stir the ingredients up a bit. List the facts of the case on a sheet of paper. List what you think your options are. Put a draft of what you are trying to write together. Jot down ten presentation points.

Step Four—Let The Ideas Simmer

Go to sleep. Let some time pass. Incubate it. Cook it. Trust it. Relax. Let the ideas simmer.

If you have others whom you work with or live with, have them join in. Get them cooking it too. Sometimes, just talking about something will trigger your thinking. Maybe there is something you can *cook* for them in return. Remember there is all kinds of extra incubating capacity out there.

How about your staff, that's what ya pay'em for, he said to no one in particular.

Step Five—Serve

When you wake up, when you come back to it, your incubator is likely ready to serve. The incubated solution, the better idea, emerges.

In essence, steps one to four are the same as chopping up the ingredients for the chile, adding the soup, celery, tomatoes and all the other ingredients and throwing them in the pot.

If you were to serve your solution right after preparation, it will be fine (the chile would be acceptable, a la the blue cup). However, if you let your solution, the report, the alternatives, the presentation, *simmer* (a la the red cup), your solution, report, your presentation will inevitably be better, richer, more textured, simply because the brain had an opportunity to incubate.

What many times may seem to be a muddled mess the day before is far clearer when we sleep on it. A problem that appeared not to have a solution amazingly has one. A presentation that was going to be so-so, takes on a new life. And why? Because the brain was busy simmering, incubating; generating new ways of coming at it; gelling new thoughts around it, distilling, coming up with new ways to deal with it.

Our challenge then is to proactively activate this existing feature of our WorldProcessor to let it work its magic.

Using Your Incubator

There are all kinds of daily uses for our incubator.

Improving Your Product

If you need to submit a report, give a speech, or prepare for anything, *get started early*. Give it time to incubate. If a one-page summary needs to be submitted tomorrow, write it today without regard to quality. Just get something down. Inevitably, when you revisit it tomorrow morning, you can enhance it tenfold before you submit it simply because you *chose* to get a head start. You started your brain working on it, you slept on it and it *cooked* overnight. Guaranteed, Counselor said, bearing in mind he was not the guaranteeing type, do this, he continued, and your results, the quality of your products, will improve.

To Better Understand A Problem

The symptoms of a problem tend to split out from the real core issue when we incubate, he pressed on. Like how a nice roast of beef falls off the bone when you cook it just right, he told us. The real issue presents itself in a way that might not have been clear at the start.

So incubate your problems. The *real* issues will emerge.

To Consider An Alternative

So too, with time and incubation, do alternate ways of coming at things miraculously begin to present themselves.

To Put Us More At Ease As We Work Through It

The incubator yields peace of mind because when we are actively incubating, we know that we have the issue, the situation, under control. Progress is being made. We're *cooking* it and we know we have had success with this process before. When the time comes, we will have worked it out!

Incubating produces a certain calm. We *have* things under control.

To Put Things In Perspective

Sometimes when we first hear about something or see something happen, it takes on gargantuan proportion. By giving what happened time to incubate, it comes more clearly into perspective.

The magnitude of what happened or what was said becomes relative to what we have seen before. We can therefore, figure out if it was *truly* significant or significant merely because it happened most recently.

Deploying the Incubator for this purpose is akin to invoking the Twenty-Four Hour Rule, a rule that tells us to give ourselves twenty-four hours to percolate or incubate anything major. By so doing, we give ourselves time to stack *it*—the deal, the offer, the behaviour—up against what we have seen before. It also allows us to determine if it is really as good as we first thought or really as bad. The Incubator helps with perspective.

Catching The Output

I am not sure how you will react to this, he said, but the output of your Incubator is not always that controllable. We may need to send that part of it back to the manufacturer because the Incubator gives us *little surprises*.

You never know when your Incubator will *produce*. You never know when that new solution or creative or better idea is going to just come *popping out*. You need to be ready when the Incubator is done incubating; you need be ready to catch its output at all times.

He then issued to each of us a small device. It was a little pad of paper with a pen affixed to it. It rested inside a pocket protector that had velcro on the back with a really small battery-powered light hooked up to it. He called this contraption an IOC, Incubator Output Collector. He told us it could be used at night.

He advised *us* that he was seeking a patent on it. We advised *him* that he should seriously consider seeking medical attention.

His worst fear, he said, was to lie in bed at night when an incubated solution would pop and he wouldn't be prepared. He told us this had actually happened, saying so in real horror.

The things he worried about...

When our *eurekas* are ready, we *have* to be ready, he almost panicked.

You see, he went on like the mad scientist that he was, this combined pen, paper, velcro, light and a pocket protector contraption is your Incubator Output Collector. It hooks up to your PJ's. It'll save your ideas! Anytime! Day or night!, he enthused.

Don't you feel relieved? he exaggerated. Again.

Yes, of course! We were trying to get him to calm down. We thought he was going to have a conniption. And we didn't even know what a conniption was.

But *he* was the doctor, so we figured we were OK.

You *must* carry your IOC with you at all times because you never know when the oven bell in your mind is going to go ding.

What?

Ding. He really did say *ding*.

He went on to confess that, for him anyway, when the ideas he was incubating were done cooking, when the solutions were ready, the timing of which he clearly couldn't control, an audible *ding* would happen. The noise he figured somehow came out of his ears. And it would happen to him constantly, any time. Day or night. Uncontrollable. No matter where he was. It was most embarrassing when he was at meetings. Ding. And people would look right at him.

He was serious. We thought.

Embarrassing. *That's* why I wear ear muffs to bed, he said, once again, giving us *way* too much detail. To muffle the ding when his ideas were finished incubating so that he wouldn't wake his wife, he explained. Meetings were one thing and the ear muffs might have affected his credibility, he said, but he felt his wife should at *least* be able to sleep if an idea came to him in the middle of the night.

He *swore* his *timer* had gone off before and that other people could hear it!

When he told us *that*, the servers gave him one look, and quickly vacated the room. We gave it some thought, too, but our old buddy couldn't be left alone.

His wife later told us he would always awaken early. Christmas morning awake. Excited. Thinking, dreaming and constantly scribbling. Fidgeting with his idea collector and adjusting his ear muffs. She never let on that he'd awakened her. She would just smile to herself and roll over, thankful that he had *learned* to love life. And if he heard dings, she winked when she told us, that was just fine with her!

Old Sayings

So the sayings *sleep on it, time heals all* and *things'll look better in the morning* now make all the more sense. Why? Because there appears to be substance behind the sayings. While we sleep, the brain is hard at work, giving the idea time to incubate.

Our Task

Our task, then, is to give the brain something to work with, give it something we've been struggling with. Read that report and sleep on it. See what happens. The brain will provide us with different ways of looking at something when we later come back to it.

Most times, what appears to be insurmountable on Monday gives way to a workable solution by Friday. I simply suggest we help our brains along. Load stuff in that you want simmered and incubated. Let your Incubator work its magic and strap your IOC on cause ya never know when it's going to start producing.

He smiled.

We smiled.

We all took a break.

the builder

I t was hard to imagine and even more difficult to picture, but Counselor next walked in as a lacrosse player. We couldn't help but chuckle. That is, until we looked into his eyes.

His outfit consisted of a pair of old beaten up red shorts, his old jersey, number 9, a leather helmet and the stick he used in his playing days. He was somehow standing a little straighter now, somehow a little taller now. And even though it was starting to get late, he *continued* to be energized, and so, too, were we.

And the lacrosse stick? It was clearly handcrafted, filed down at the top and also on the shaft. The shooter strings were still in it, the leather still moist.

And with the way he held that stick and with the fire burning in those eyes, you could tell that our Counselor had been a *player*.

He was ready to tell us about leadership and what it takes to build a team. And we were ready to listen.

He told us that he was not an expert on leading,

because that would be presumptuous. He was, however, fully qualified on *being* lead, he told us, so it would be from *that* perspective that he would speak.

The C on his jersey and the way he could inspire somehow told us otherwise, but Counselor was being Counselor, so we decided to let it pass.

He told us that he had seen common threads between those he admired as leaders. Similarly, he had been on and seen successful teams. Some common characteristics ran through them as well.

And the lacrosse outfit? That was from the best team he had ever been on. And why the sports metaphor?

It had been his experience that much could be transferred from the field of sport, to the topics of leadership and team building. It was his contention that all we needed to be more effective as a leader and team builder, was to look at the best leaders we had ever had and look at the best teams we were ever on and distill up the characteristics of each. We could then apply what we learned to the group situations we now place ourselves in.

Counselor liked to keep things simple. And this was a good way to look at leadership and a good way to look at team building.

LEADERSHIP

Before he listed the characteristics, he warned us that this was a *hybrid* list, his *want-to-be* list; a list of the positive traits of inspirational leaders he had had the opportunity to observe. It was something to shoot for as a leader.

Difficult, no make that darn near impossible, for any one person to attain, he confessed, but a target nevertheless.

He then walked us through his list...

They Were Credible

You didn't always like to hear what they had to say, but you knew that what they said was legitimate and to be believed. You trusted what they said.

They Role Modeled The Behaviour They Expected From You

There was no *do as I say* in them. It was very much *do as I do*.

They Were Consistent

On a day to day basis, we knew what to expect.

They Were Human And Made Mistakes

But if they did, and it affected you, an apology would be forthcoming.

They Initiated

They made things happen. They were proactive as opposed to reactive.

They Were Approachable

While there was never any doubt who was in charge, if there was something that you *had* to discuss, you never felt as though you were an inconvenience.

They Were Considerate And Polite

It didn't seem to matter who you were, opening doors and even serving *you* coffee, as opposed to you waiting on them, seemed to come naturally. The more senior they became, the harder they worked to make you feel that you were someone equally contributing to the outcome.

They Led

When it was clear a leader was needed, in times of uncertainty or confusion, they took the bull by the horns and led.

They Communicated

If something needed to be said, they said it. If it was important, they said it face to face.

They Were Confident in Themselves

Not cocky, confident. And that confidence inspired confidence in those they led.

They Were Enthusiastic

They liked doing what they were doing. They were *pumped* and it rubbed off.

They Were Resources and Resourceful

They were there when you needed information; they knew their stuff. And somehow they also found a way to get you the equipment you needed to do your job. They were quite prepared to head out on a limb to get you what you needed.

They Intuitively Understood Context

They seemed to intuitively understand that they were largely responsible for creating the *job context* their direct reports, the team members, would operate in. They knew that they were largely responsible for the mood, the culture, and ultimately the results of the *work unit* they led.

They knew that they couldn't and shouldn't do the jobs of their team members. However, they knew their main responsibility was to create an atmosphere where these people could do their best work, where they could work their magic.

They Made You Feel Important

They pointed the big picture out to you and how you were integral to making that big picture complete.

They Dished Out Consequences

If you did well, you heard about it. On the flipside, if you consistently made mistakes, you paid the price. They made the tough hire-fire decisions, when the tough decisions had to be made.

They Knew How To Build A Team

The best leaders knew how to build a team.

BUILDING A TEAM

He then switched gears to building a team.

Think with me if you will, he implored, think back to your past. Think back to the best team you were ever on, he encouraged.

Think of the faces, what you went through together. He walked up and got right in our faces. Think about it. Remember the feeling.

He didn't quite grab us by the shoulders and shake us into recall but he was thinking about it. He was now in full *inspire mode*.

Do you have it? he asked. Do you have that team in mind?

Do *you*?

We did.

Excellent.

Here were the characteristics of the best team I was ever on, he said.

See how it squares with yours. My sense is that what made my team work and what likely made your team work can also make the teams that we are now on—work, non-work, volunteer or otherwise—work as well!

Clear Goals

Everybody knew what we were after and where we were headed. There was clearly a *higher purpose* that held us together and to which we would subordinate personal glory. These goals also gave us reasons to resolve conflicts. Focusing on the common good made us realize that at some point we needed to solve the problem and move on.

Clear Roles

Everybody knew their role, what was expected, and their part in the whole scheme of things.

Communication

Everybody knew what was going on. If something was important we got together.

Clear Expectations

Everyone knew what was expected of them and of each other.

Mutual Respect

We respected the talents, skills, but most of all, the efforts of others.

There Were Consequences

There were consequences, *clear and direct*, tied to our actions. If we delivered, we were rewarded. If we didn't, we were either off the team or our floor time was reduced.

Strong Leadership

While there was pride at stake and peer pressure to perform, there is no doubt that we were also led.

Stoked

We were tremendously *enthused* by what we were doing.

Successful

We did well. We got results.

Tough Competition

There was tough competition. We therefore had *common enemies*. Sure there were things that bugged us inside, but we knew where the real battles were, what our real purpose was, and it was *not* to fight with each other.

Recognition

We were recognized individually and as a team.

Admission

It was tough to gain admission to this club. It wasn't easy to get on this team. People knew it was an honour to be part of it.

Worked Hard and Played Hard

There was a sense of camaraderie. We worked hard together but we also meticulously planned events where we could also play hard together, as well.

Shared Experiences

Simply by being together as a team, we began to share life experiences with one another, our families, friends and loved ones. Over time, we naturally grew together because we had *shared experiences*. The larger the team, the larger the family, the longer it takes, but the camaraderie eventually happens.

Mutual Trust—No Dropped Balls

While we all had our individual roles, it was also clear and expected that when one of us was overloaded, we would pitch in for the other guy. If a ball was between us, a job in no man's land, the norm was to go for it, as opposed to looking at each other and letting it hit the ground.

We developed mutual trust over time. You bail me out, I bail you out. You just do it. You don't question it.

Cool Uniforms

And finally, as you can see, he said, we had what we thought were really cool uniforms, past glories snapping back.

We thought we looked great, he once again beamed, and then laid down his stick.

the arsenal

A nd he reappeared *instantly*.
He now appeared in his best four-star General's uniform.

Eighteen down, three to go. Lets suck it up, people. Not far to go now, he reported, hands on his hips, reflective shades reflecting, as he surveyed his *theatre*...

It's a jungle out there, ladies and gentlemen, he declared. And during your stay here, he went on, eyes fixed straight ahead in their best military glare, you will want to get other people to do things, your kids to make their beds, your employees to go that extra mile. Other people will try to influence *your* behaviour, as well.

And to do this, you can deploy specific tools and tactics to make sure this happens. These tactics will also be deployed *on* you. You, therefore, need to know what's *in your arsenal*: the tactics and tools we can use to influence the behaviour of others, and the tools and tactics that others will use to influence us, consciously or unconsciously.

Again, as with most of our Attitools, we simply raise

these ways of wielding power and influencing to the level of consciousness to increase our understanding and to better enable us to manage and recognize them.

He then turned it up to five star volume and tone...

Some of these tools of power and influence are *decent* and frankly, some *aren't pretty*. But my purpose here is not to judge. My *mission* is to equip you fully with the arsenal you need, the knowledge you need, to properly win some of these battles; to properly defend yourself; to get others to do things and to see how others are trying to influence you.

These tactics are neither bad nor good, he said. They may even all have a place and a time. The reality, though, is that they exist so you'd better darn well know they are out there! He paused, pulling in a huge breath as if he were a balloon inflating itself.

We then knew *why*, as the exhale began...

Aaaaaaaaaaaaaaaaaaaaaattttteeeeennnnnnn,sssssssssssss sssssssssssssssshhhhhhhhhuuuuuuunnnnnnnnnnn!

We all stood and saluted. We had to! What else are you going do after that anyway? He also very much expected it. It was kind of a ritual. But when he saluted back, he pulled his hand back a little too quick and popped himself in the beak. It took him a second or two to *come to*, but as *his* lights came back on, so, too, did the lights outside.

We hadn't realized it, but it was getting *really* late now. But he couldn't have cared less. Actually, he couldn't have cared *more*. That's why we were still there. There were still a few more things he needed us to know and he wasn't about to let up now.

Gimme ten!!!

Massive groan from the crowd this time.

And just as he said that, he dropped to the floor. Five one-handed push-ups on each side in a matter of seconds and he was back on his feet. A little red in the face, was he, but still standing nevertheless. Now *there* was a Pracellerator!

He had saved his best for last. Or just about his best, just about for last...

We didn't bother with the push ups, instead we gave him a standing ovation.

He then went on to introduce us to the tactics people can use to influence others, an overview of our sources of power and influence.

He stayed with the military theme but made it clear that leaders, managers, parents, co-workers or coaches could and might use any or all of these tactics, knowingly or unknowingly. He also pointed out that many of these tactics were not *age or hierarchy* specific. He directed this point in particular to the younger ones in the classroom but it applied to all of us.

Be aware, he said, that you can make *much more of a difference* early in your career than you might think. No matter where you sit in the hierarchy or how long-in-the-tooth you are, you can add tremendous value and make significant headway simply by being aware of and deploying some of these tactics.

Here is what he said.

Each of us will have different impressions of these tactics. People who are skilled at influencing others, however, know about each one of these. I therefore introduce these to you for your awareness, for you to decide which ones you choose to use, and to also be aware when each is being used on you!

I do not wish to make our behaviour mechanical. I do, however, wish to make how we and others behave more recognizable, understandable and changeable. Sometimes we deploy tactics that simply do not work, tactics that are easy to deploy, but ineffective in the long run. My purpose is to help us *see the errors in our ways*, he said militarily, for our benefit and those we work and live with.

Be aware, however, the General was back, that there will be instances where the use of force may be necessary. We knew he was joking, in a way.

Our methods of influencing others, our sources of power, our tactics available to deploy in our battle to influence people are as follows, he bellowed in his best General turned Drill Sergeant!

Our Position

As General, I am at the top of the hierarchy, he said. And by virtue of my position, I have the authority to lead.

Our position serves as a source of power and influence, as does our ability to provide rewards and punish.

What We Can Do For Them—Our Capacity To Provide Rewards

As General, as leader, I can influence your behaviour by rewarding you. I pay you. I can raise your pay. I can also promote you. Equally, or more importantly, I can provide non-monetary rewards. I can praise your work. I can compliment your bravery.

What We Can Do To Them—Our Capacity To Punish

Conversely as General, I can make your life Heck, he

commanded. John Wayne and George C. Scott all wrapped up into one, he said.

I can punish, demote, suspend. I can even throw you into solitary, he threatened.

Who We Can Be or Are Connected To—By Virtue of Whose Ear We Have

I happen also to be personally connected to The President and the head of the Joint Chiefs of Staff, he pretended. At a moment's notice, I can *be in touch*. I can make things happen through my network, through my contacts.

I can make things happen for you people in this war! he declared, chest out, fake metals flailing, plastic monocle popping onto the floor.

He was doing his best here.

You *may* be able to influence others, whether you mean to or not, by virtue of who you are connected to, who you know, or who others perceive you can connect them to.

What We Can Get For Them—By Virtue of What We Can Dole Out

This is a form of reward, but there is a subtle difference.

I have also secured access to additional rations and the best guns and artillery, he boasted. We feed our people good, he purposefully misspoke to sound more authoritative; and we keep'em alive! As a result, my unit attracts only the best and the brightest.

He looked around at all of us, implying that maybe we were part of his elite team of commandos. I must say, we all sat up a little straighter again. There was no slumping in *that* room. At least not for long anyway.

What We Can Teach Them—By Virtue of What We Know

This is one of the more powerful ways we can influence others, he prefaced. You youngsters, listen up, he implored. You don't have to be a leader to influence others using this tactic. You can even hierarchically, be at entry level.

I have fought in four wars, led over three hundred thousand troops and never lost a one. I have studied war strategy at the Pentagon for over fifty years, he stretched. Ladies and gentlemen, I know war!, he decreed.

He stepped out of character briefly to make this point:

What we *know*, the expertise we have or can develop, around:

- our job
- our craft
- our industry
- our market share
- our competitors
- our marketplace
- our client's needs and wants
- our trade associations
- our industry issues

whether we are twenty-one or fifty-one has tremendous value and has great influencing capacity.

We become an extremely valuable resource by virtue of what we know. By virtue of what we know, we add value to those who associate with us.

And this, he bellowed from the highest mountain, clearly reiterating what we had talked about with the

Shingle, is a *highly controllable dimension* of our value to others and our ability to influence outcomes, most notably, our career progress. No one controls what we know about our industry or about our job but us! It is not age specific nor does it matter where we sit in the hierarchy. And if that sounds a little mercenary, he cautioned, so be it; it's a jungle out there, he said, half joking, half not.

Here is the hard reality, ladies and gentlemen. If I think you can either save some of my other people's lives or help me win this war, if you can add value, you are on my team.

And I don't really care how old ya are or what your job is. Why? Because *you're* good, you make *me* look good! And *I* get another star. I become a seventeen star general, he kind-of smiled.

What value we can add to others' situations is a key determinant of whether or not we can influence what they decide to do.

He was operating at a pretty base level here, but he was right on the money. He was pulling no punches.

Whether We Include Them

You, you, you, and you, he was careful to point to every one of us. I need your advice! Over here, on the double. The *rest* of you stand easy.

Imagine, he said, if I had done that for real. Think of how you would feel if you were included, and think about how you would feel if you were *not*.

As leaders, we can swing sentiment largely by *how* and *who* we include in our decision making processes. This source of power and way of either motivating others or demonstrating them is many times overlooked.

I highlight it as a rather sharp instrument in our arsenal. Being included or being excluded, either on purpose or by accident, leaves an indelible mark, so handle with care. Whether by omission or by commission, we draw conclusions from whether we get included or not.

As a coach, or as a leader then, we must not be insensitive to this dimension's impact. Careful attention to who is included and when, and who is involved and when, can mean the difference when it comes time to call on the troops; when we need'em to suck it up! Fairly treated, *they're with ya*! Unfairly treated, real or perceived, *they're agin' ya*, he observed.

So how or whether the troops feel they have been involved is one dimension they will factor in when you call on them to take up arms and go to the front! So be aware of it.

How We Treat Them—Through Our Force Of Personality

I am a humble man, from humble beginnings, our General began, and I am here to serve you. I will go to the end of the earth for you, my troops! he said.

Word had seeped back from the front lines of a General Counselor had once known, his charisma, his work ethic, generosity and his ability to inspire. And this capacity to lift others through sheer force of personality, is the crux of yet another way to influence the behaviour of others.

People will follow you, yes because of what you know and yes because of your position; but also they will follow you and *put out* for you because of the *way* you lead; by the way you *inspire*!, he inspired – many times through the intangibles:

- charisma
- attitude
- outlook
- demeanor
- the way you carry yourself
- your reputation
- how you treat people
- even how you look

Your Arsenal

So there ladies and gentlemen is your *arsenal*, the array of weaponry that can and will be used in the battle of life. It is important to point out that we use all these ways of influencing others, not only in leader-follower relationships, but parent and child, co-worker to co-worker, volunteer to volunteer instances, as well.

You can also clearly see that some of these are far more effective than others. However, he reiterated, different people respond to different things.

He then stepped out of his General...

You are not naive people, he began, and let drift over the audience to let us know he was leveling with us again. We were back into Reality 101, which we appreciated from time to time.

My advice to you, he said, is to be aware of all of these ways of influencing behaviour. Perhaps even download this menu of options into your WorldProcessor for possible deployment.

As with any of these tools, though, I would caution against misuse, overuse or insincere use. The reality is that we need to be aware of when they are being deployed, again either consciously or unconsciously, on us. Recognizing clearly what is *incoming* gives us choices. If what is incoming is well intended, we act accordingly. If it is not, heat shields go up and we then respond accordingly.

By being able to X-*ray* and see through the use of these tactics, by understanding what is happening, we are better able to respond. By *seeing through* these tactics, we are able to put the antennae up, to unbundle what is happening. We see things more clearly. We make better decisions on how to act, react and respond. We are better able to step back a bit, objectively, coolly detached, using our adult, to see them for what they are; tactics, part of an influencing arsenal.

Recommended Position A on this, troops, is wide eyed and receptive while maintaining our awareness, he said. Some call this position Rose Coloured Safety Glasses. As relationships deepen, our *guards* can be relieved of duty. The *safety* part can be removed.

Most times, we don't need *any* analysis. We just live. We give the praise, accept the compliment, accept the criticism. Nothing more. Nothing less. But as leaders, parents, team members and new recruits, it serves us well to at least be aware of what we have, and what others have, in the arsenal!

And that, he declared standing bolt upright, is what I learned when I served alongside General George (pause) S. (longer pause) Patton (longest pause). He stared directly ahead as he saluted and dropped straight down for ten more one handers...

And then......he just laid there...

He then paused, collecting himself, trying hard to haul

his carcass back up off the floor for the umpteenth time, looking more than a little dusty, and way more than a little disheveled.

Counselor had battled and we didn't know if he was going to make it.

But then he started to move, the last two to go.

the freezer

C ounselor introduced this next to last *way of looking at things* with a sort of curiosity in his voice. He was pensive now, reflective. We were almost at the end.

He told us his buddies at Mission Control had cleared us for landing, but there was a bit more work to do before *reentry*.

He then began...

There is a place, he said, where we only occasionally find ourselves. This *place* is unique and solemn. It is recognizable by its capacity to block out anything else that is happening in our lives and for its capacity to consume. We remember the detail. This *place* is a moment when nothing else really matters. It is a moment when we are locked in without distractions. And when these moments happen, they are remarkable, and truly unforgettable!

So, in the spirit of trying to get the most out of life, rather than just let these moments happen, why not look for ways to make them happen more often and look for ways to enjoy them more fully when they just come about.

We listened intently as he carefully proceeded...

I introduce you to the *Freezer* as a way of helping us relish, cherish and appreciate *moments* when they occur. There are certain of life's events that have their own way of activating our senses. Weddings and funerals come most to mind, he said. But there will be other *moments*. We will know them when they arrive, but we can heighten these experiences by *freezing* them.

Having a Moment

As with most of the ways we learned we could look at things that day, we also discovered that having a moment is a matter of choice. We can *all* make this choice; to lock in on a moment, to experience something to the fullest, to burn it in our memory, to keep it with us for all times.

How Do We Activate the Freezer?

So how do we activate this new feature of our WP? There are three steps, he said.
• we switch off our Woptou Scanner
• we click on to our child
• we make an active choice to settle in, to *lock* in, to block out the world and focus

When Are We Having a Moment?

And how will we really know when we are having a moment? Well, Counselor said, we have all had lots of moments. We just didn't call them that, at the time. Here based on my experience, he said, are ways that we might *know* when we are at those rarefied places called moments:
• when absolutely nothing matters except what we are

experiencing

- when our senses almost automatically switch over to *full receive*
- when we are in awe
- when time stands still
- when things slow down
- when we put our pens down and just take it all in
- when we've let our guard down
- when we get *the chills*
- when we feel connected even if we aren't and even if we can't be
- when we get absolutely and completely *drawn in*
- when we are not afraid to close our eyes so we can listen better
- when we are most thankful
- when we are most humble
- when we are completely focussed
- when we are in *full child*

And moments can just sneak up on us, he said, like:

When your young son looks you square in the eye, through that incongruous steel cage over his face, all the way across the ice, while he sits on the end of the bench where he's *been* sitting for a while. And right out of nowhere, the glove on his right hand comes off and he gives you a six-year -old's *thumbs up* to let you know that he'll be OK. And you're stunned because you didn't even know he was looking at *you*; then, you melt because while everybody else is playing their hearts out, *his* heart is breaking. But at this age, he has decided to be *strong*. And while you just want to hold him, *he* is holding *you*.

That, he said is a *moment*!

Or when your daughter's Christmas Choir is singing and you think of your Mom. And when you watch your daughter sing with all her might, you realize how much she looks like your Mom when she sang with all her might. And you think of how much your Mom would have desperately loved to be there if she were still alive to watch her granddaughter sing and you shed a tear of remembrance, of a little regret, but mostly of fond memories. And you're not really thinking about what anybody else thinks.

That, *too*, is a moment!

And now you know why it is important to catch them, to *freeze* them, to have moments, he said, turning away a little as he tried to collect himself one more time, while having a hard time; having a hard time because it was clear he had just shared his deepest feelings with you in hopes that you would learn to see what he had learned to see.

And in hindsight, we came to know, that *that, too*, was a moment.

the backpatter

E yes just a little red, he turned back to us to finish off. It was now time to go.

By now, we were all wasted. Counselor was too, although he'd never admit it. He was stubborn that way. He was stubborn most ways. He had high expectations of himself and expected no less from us. He would see this through to the finish.

He was out of his General's outfit and back into his lacrosse uniform. He'd even strapped his old leather helmet back on. He was going out *his way*!

He looked at us and we looked at him. We were all smiling the knowing kind of smile that grows out of having worked really hard together and having *accomplished* something. We had all done our best, and maybe not gotten it just right, but still, pretty close!

Outta gas? he asked.

For now, we said.

Me too, he finally confessed.

It was dark outside. Just as it was when we began the

day. But somehow, things had never seemed brighter.

Before you go, the parental eyebrow flashing as one or two people had started to pack up before it was time, wresting control of the room one last time, there is one last tool I would like to introduce you to, he said.

One more?

One more...

Have you ever noticed how tough it is to scratch your own back? he began.

It's tough to reach, a little awkward, he leaned back as he attempted the contort...

That's why they invented the backscratcher, he wheezed, having pulled one out of his *tool box.*

You see how it works?

We did so indeed.

The BackPatter

Well, the same thing holds true with this new device I invented. It's called the *BackPatter*, he announced proudly.

The BackPatter can be installed in your WP, right beside the BackSide Kicker that seems to have come pre-installed, he smiled. We tend to use the BackSide Kicker way more than we ought to and our BackPatter not enough!

Did I tell you I called the Patent Office?

Absolutely! we fibbed, trying to avoid yet another tangent.

Confused, because he was sure he hadn't told us, he nevertheless pressed on...

You use the BackPatter to give yourself credit, to pat yourself on the back!

The appropriate times for the BackPatter, he got back on track, are when you have given it your best shot, and maybe you got it just right and maybe you didn't, but the point is you gave it *everything* you had.

The BackPatter is designed for *just* that time. When you deserve a pat on the back but you don't see anybody there willing or able to do it. It's just you. When the back you have been carrying all the weight on could use a bit of a pat.

It is exactly at that point that you click on to your BackPatter. Times such as:

- right around midnight and you have just put that important report on your boss's desk and maybe you couldn't get the graphics to look perfect but it is a darn fine report nevertheless and maybe everybody else has long since gone home,

    Or,

- when you are miles from home, have studied like crazy and just written the exam, and maybe you didn't get perfect but you know you did well and you can't get through to your parents on the phone,

    Or,

- maybe after you've worked really hard to prepare your speech and just given it, and maybe you lost your spot once, but *you* knew that you went that ten extra miles to do your best; and while it wasn't perfect or somebody else's best, it was *your* best, and you deserve to give yourself credit,

    Or,

- maybe it was when you started working the second you rolled out of bed and hadn't stopped until right now, and

not one soul has said thank you yet today,
Or
- when you've gotten yourself over to the Driver's Seat, taken control and done all that you possibly can

All of these times are perfect times for the BackPatter!
The BackPatter reminds us *that we did good*!

We savour our accomplishments and learn to rely on ourselves. We celebrate our accomplishments and learn to rest along the way.

Someday Becomes Today

Only when we get there will we be truly happy gives way to *I'll be satisfied with today. Strive, strive never arrive* gives way to *today was a good day and while we didn't get it all right, we made a lot of headway.*

Being satisfied only when we get there gives way to enjoying the ride. *Someday I'll be happy* gives way to *Someday's Here.*

Counselor believed so much in trying to enjoy the present that as a personal reminder, the family decision had been made to name the family yacht, Someday's Here. In true Counselor fashion, though, the family yacht was actually a previously-enjoyed fourteen-footer. But he didn't care, it was a yacht to *him*!

What I Want Most

What I most want with the BackPatter, he told us, is for us to acquire the ability to give ourselves credit when credit is due. To self-congratulate when it is deserved. To self-accept even when it wasn't perfect. To validate internally, to self-energize, to trust in ourselves, and rely on *ourselves* for the definition of a *job well done*. We know when we've done our best and deserve credit.

We are the judge *and* we are the jury. Only *we* know the hours, the sweat and the pain. And so with the BackPatter, we learn to not look out, but rely on what's within; to congratulate ourselves accordingly, when we have done the best that we can.

A Pause in the Journey

This way of looking at things allows for a pause in the journey, a place to rest for a while. To rejuvenate and re-energize. It is the comma in the sentence, the service centre just off the road.

When you've given it all you have, he pointed out, think about what you've done, not what you haven't. A prime example is today! You actually made it to the end! And only two slid into coma, which is *way* better than my average, better than my *was*. He smiled...

Think about what you've accomplished as you leave here, not about what you have not. Think about how far you've come, not about how far you have to go. Think about time left and forget any time lost.

Because if we *choose* to look through *those* eyes, talking as much now to himself as he was to us, if we *choose* to do *that*, *then* we will *choose* to be happy!

And that, he concluded, deserves a pat on the back.

He then turned to face us, to finish off the day.

the beginning

A nd that day? What a day it was! What a *life*! And as I
close the book on what I learned from Counselor, as I
look back over the past ten years, here is what I discovered.

I discovered that I *always* have choices. I just hadn't
seen it that way before. I also learned that, in fact, *what I
believe* and *how I look at things* drives directly *how I
behave*. And that it doesn't hurt now and again, to revisit
what I believe and *how I look at things*. To upgrade my
WorldProcessor, to see if how I am looking at the world is
producing the results I want.

I realized the *power* of looking at things differently, of
deploying Counselor's Attitools. They helped with my perspective, my self-acceptance, my acceptance of others, my
optimism and my sense for *what is possible*. And yes
Counselor, I even learned to shut off my Woptou Scanner
long enough to *have a moment*.

I took his advice to heart and have tried to put it to
good use.

I'm still *trying*, just ask my family, but I'm hopefully a

little better than I was before. I still make mistakes, lots of them, but I've also made headway, far beyond what I had ever expected.

I learned that making headway feeds on itself. *The more I do, the more I am able to do*!

I have learned that my mood and my outlook are *also* my *choice*.

And Counselor? I don't know if he ever *really* knew anyone at Mission Control or if he really had a boat, but my guess is he probably did play a little lacrosse and I *do* know that he had a zest for life. He was full of wonder and maybe a little full of some other stuff too. But that made Counselor Counselor.

He was a kid in a grown-up's body. But that, *too*, was a choice. And of that, he could not have been more proud. And for that, I could not be more grateful.

And now that I look back on it, that day for me was just the start point, the beginning of a lifelong process of looking at things in new, clearer ways. And things haven't really *looked* the same since.

The Very End

And the very end of the day? I'll never forget how he wound our session down that Saturday those ten years ago.

Still in his lacrosse outfit, stick, gloves and helmet, and drenched from having spent all he had, he was a sight to behold.

To think, in the morning he was this *distinguished gentlemen* and now he was our *trusted friend*. Someone who desperately wanted nothing more for us than peace of mind.

And right at the end? He actually thanked *us* for putting up with *him*. He confessed his self-doubt, and his nervousness in front of a crowd. He also said he never knew if he'd done a good enough job, but that he was satisfied and at peace knowing he had tried his hardest.

And at the very end, he left us with his last thought, his motto, what he wanted us *most* to remember...

You know, he said, as he met each of our eyes one last time, my is *still* isn't my *could be* yet.

You could see him getting all consternated again...

But you know what, he said as he began now to drift away, it is *better* than my *was*!

And with that, he thanked us *again*. Head a little down, he turned, and walked slowly out of the room. A little lost in thought, as he always was, but looking forward now, to going home.

As I Close This Book

And Counselor?...as I close *your* book, just so you know?

Your best was *much* more than good enough!

Our *is* is now far better than our *was*.

So with a quiet salute, we thank you, Sir.

And for all of us, Good-bye.

glossary of terms

Analaphor – a way of describing something that takes *complete* liberty with the language and that lives somewhere between a metaphor and an analogy.

Angster – one who stews too much.

Angsting – to angst. A new verb. Angsting is advanced *stewing*.

Arsenal – the *tools* and *tactics* of power and influence. Sounds pretty military.

Attitools – filters through which we can view things, ways of looking at things. These can be installed in our WorldProcessors.

Attitooldom – what we can graduate in to.

BackPatter – an underutilized tool that we ought to deploy more often. It is what we should use when we've done our best and deserve a pat on the back.

BackSideKicker – what we use far too often.

Brakes – what we use to help us stop looking at things counter-productively.

Builder – a tool we deploy to help us understand leadership and to help us build teams.

Calculator – a tool that serves as a reminder, as if we need one, that our financial well-being affects our overall well-being. The Calculator comes with suggestions on how to improve our financial well-being.

Clicker – a tool we can use to help us manage the volume of the voice inside.

Could Be – where we would like to be.

Consternated – a state of unknowing that is difficult to express, difficult to pass.

Counselorspeak – what happens when we take complete liberty with the language.

DDD Alarm – the alarm that goes off when we begin to seize-up in the face of change. Danger! Danger! Danger!

Deeeeluxe Clicker – a tool that helps us manage not only the volume of the voice inside but also, its content and tone.

Drainer – energy depleter, mindshare hog.

Driver's Seat – a way of looking at things that helps us learn how to be more in control of our own destinies.

Extension Cord – a way of looking at things that might help us stick around longer.

Freezer – helps us stay in and enjoy *moments*.

Gear Shifter – proactively choosing which of three ways of communicating and relating, the parent, the adult or the child, we wish to deploy given the situation.

Incubator – what we activate to *proactively* generate ideas and new ways of looking at things.

Incubator Output Collector – a device designed to catch good ideas whenever they *pop*.

Is – where we are now.

Jacket (a.k.a Reverser) – suggests that questions are in some cases not really questions at all; *rather* they are statements.

Knife – a tool to slice our lives up into their component parts to isolate the ingredients in our recipe that *energize* and to isolate the ones that *drain*.

Locus of Control – the extent to which we believe we control events in our lives; understanding we use to help us get into the Driver's Seat.

Mindshare – the amount of attention something takes, what we spend our time thinking about.

Mover – an action planning methodology to help us close the gap between our *is* and our *could be*.

Newtoning – reasoning logically, using physics as a basis for reasoning.

Overbehave – overreact.

POMTGR – our peace of mind to grief ratio; a measure of our overall sense of well-being.

Positivity – the opposite of negativity.

Pracellerate – finding someone who has done something we would like to do and learning from them. Pracellerating flattens the learning curve.

Pracellerator – a role model, an inspiration, someone from whom we can learn; what our Pracell-Scanner looks for.

Pracell-Scanner – what we activate to find Pracellerators.

PreFlight Checklist – a tool to assess our readiness, willingness and capacity to make change.

Query Flipper – what we use to decide if a question is really a statement.

Re-Attitool – to look at things differently, to look at things through different lenses.

Seat Belt – a tool to understand how we make and break habits.

Self-Finetunement – the daily efforts we make to close the gap between our is and could be. The fine-tuning activities we undertake everyday to more closely align our personal circumstances with what we know works for us in terms of job content, job context and life context.

Self-Optometrize – to change the way we look at things. Ourselves.

Self-Scanner – what we use to scan for which self; parent, adult or child, we or others have deployed.

Shingle – what we hang in our mind as a reminder that we are all really in our own business.

Slanging – purposeful mis-use of a word to make a point *real* clear. An old Western movie typically comes to mind pardner.

SLOMOE (a.k.a. Self-Loathing Muttering of Exasperation) – what sneaks out after we mis-hit a golf ball.

Triscrunching – the physical behaviour that accompanies thinking hard.

Venting Licence – a tool we use to keep it together.

Wedge – a tool we insert to help give us the time we need to make better decisions.

Wiifm Scanner (a.k.a. What's In It For Me Scanner) – what we use to assess whether or not something is worth paying attention to.

Whto Scanner (a.k.a. What Happens To Others Scanner) – what we should consider when we are assessing the impact of a habitual way we have of behaving or believing.
Wwtoo Scanner (a.k.a. What We Think Of Ourselves Scanner) – what we use to figure out how we are feeling about ourselves. This one has a wide dial because of the variances in mood and opinion we can have of ourselves.

Woptou Scanner (a.k.a. What Other People Think Of Us Scanner) – the scanner we have on, that we tend to have on too much, that tells us what we think other people think about us. We can learn to switch it off.

Wonderment - neighbouring state of the emotional state of Easygoing; where we spent time as kids and can spend time as adults, if we so choose.

WorldProcessor – the filter we use to process things. What resides between what happens to us and what we do and feel about it. It is upgradeable and is where we install our Attitools.

appendix one

SLICE OF LIFE SNAPSHOT

ERA: _____ FROM: _____ TO: _____

	WHAT WORKED	WHAT DIDN'T WORK
JOB CONTENT		
	•	•
	•	•
	•	•
	•	•
	•	•
	•	•
JOB CONTEXT		
	•	•
	•	•
	•	•
	•	•
	•	•
	•	•
LIFE CONTEXT		
	•	•
	•	•
	•	•
	•	•
	•	•
	•	•

SUMMARY THOUGHTS: _____

_____

_____

_____

SLICE OF LIFE SNAPSHOT

ERA: FROM: TO:

	WHAT WORKED	WHAT DIDN'T WORK
JOB CONTENT		
	•	•
	•	•
	•	•
	•	•
	•	•
	•	•
JOB CONTEXT		
	•	•
	•	•
	•	•
	•	•
	•	•
	•	•
LIFE CONTEXT		
	•	•
	•	•
	•	•
	•	•
	•	•
	•	•

SUMMARY THOUGHTS: _____

_____

_____

_____

SLICE OF LIFE SNAPSHOT

ERA: FROM: TO:

	WHAT WORKED	WHAT DIDN'T WORK
JOB CONTENT		
	•	•
	•	•
	•	•
	•	•
	•	•
	•	•
JOB CONTEXT		
	•	•
	•	•
	•	•
	•	•
	•	•
	•	•
LIFE CONTEXT		
	•	•
	•	•
	•	•
	•	•
	•	•
	•	•

SUMMARY THOUGHTS: _____

_____

_____

_____

_____

appendix two
GETTING TO KNOW ME BETTER WORKSHEET

WHAT SKILLS AND ABILITIES...

Do I Like Using   Am I Good At

- •   - •
- •   - •
- •   - •
- •   - •
- •   - •

WHAT SKILLS AND ABILITIES...

Do I Dislike Using   Am I Brutal At

- •   - •
- •   - •
- •   - •
- •   - •
- •   - •

appendix three

JOB CONTENT ACTION PLANNER

To start closing the gap between my job content *is* and *could be*, I need to:

Immediately:

-
-
-
-
-

Within Six Months:

-
-
-
-
-

Eventually:

-
-
-
-
-

appendix four
JOB CONTEXT ACTION PLANNER

To start closing the gap between my job context *is* and *could be*, I need to:

Immediately:
-
-
-
-
-

Within Six Months:

-
-
-
-
-

Eventually:

-
-
-
-
-

appendix five

LIFE CONTEXT ACTION PLANNER

To start closing the gap between my life context *is* and *could be*, I need to:

Immediately:

-
-
-
-
-

Within Six Months:

-
-
-
-
-

Eventually:

-
-
-
-
-

appendix six
PRACELLERATION WORKSHEET

I'd really like to...
(Complete the sentence)

Potential Pracellerators
(Those who might help)

Start

Stop

Increase

Decrease

Build

Create

Improve

Help

notes to self

_____

_____

_____

_____

_____

_____

_____

_____

_____

_____

_____

_____

_____

_____

_____

_____

_____

_____

_____

_____

_____

_____

_____

_____

_____

_____

notes to self

about the author

R ic Asselstine is short, has a shiney forehead and
a failing slap shot. He runs his own management
consulting practice in Waterloo, Ontario, Canada.

An experienced business builder, Ric has grown his
own companies and helped others build theirs. From his
own life experiences, professional training and ongoing
research, he continues to distill and evolve his understanding of why we do the things we do.

A seasoned speaker and consultant, Ric's more than
twenty years of accomplishments have taken him from "concept to boardroom" and from appearances on CTV's Canada
AM and CBC Radio to the pages of the Globe and Mail
newspaper, Macleans and Canadian Business magazines.

Holding BBA and MBA degrees, Ric lives with his
family in Waterloo, Ontario. He also lectures in communication, individual and organizational behaviour at Wilfrid
Laurier University.

Born and raised in Wallaceburg, Ontario, Ric hopes one
day to be drafted by the Toronto Maple Leafs. Having been
passed over for twenty-five years though, he is starting to
get the picture.

HOW TO REACH RIC

To discuss having Ric speak at your next event, please:

Telephone:	(519)-884-1117
Fax:	(519)-884-8452
Email	ric@attitools.com

Attitools®

MAKES A GREAT GIFT!

TO ORDER

Please rush me _____ copies of Attitools
@ CAN $18.95 _____
@ USA $14.95 _____
Postage and handling: $2.00 per book. _____

SUBTOTAL _____
Canadian Residents add 7% G.S.T. _____

TOTAL AMOUNT ENCLOSED _____

Full Name: _____

Organization: _____

Address: _____

City: _____ Province: _____

Postal Code/Zip Code: _____ Telephone: _____

Email: _____

Please make all cheques or money orders payable to
Ric Asselstine & Associates,
P.O. Box 42081, 550 King Street North, Waterloo, Ontario, N2L 6K5

Or charge my: Visa   MasterCard   American Express

Card Number _____ Expiry Date:_____

For **BULK SALES** (orders of ten or over), we offer **discounts**.
Please call, fax or email us for details. Here's how to get in touch:

Telephone: **1-877-ATT-TOOL**
Fax: **(519) 884-8452**
Email: **orders@attitools.com**

Please allow four to six weeks for delivery.
www.attitools.com